Allotment
Handbook

Allotment
Handbook

Simon Akeroyd

LONDON, NEW YORK, MUNICH,
MELBOURNE, DELHI

Project Editors   May Corfield,
                      Hilary Mandleberg
Senior Art Editor   Alison Gardner
Senior Editor   Chauney Dunford
Photography   Peter Anderson
Projects   Alexander Storch
Senior Jacket Creative   Nicola Powling
Senior Producer   Seyhan Esen
Producer, pre-production   George Nimmo
Picture Research   Susie Peachey
Managing Editor   Penny Warren
Managing Art Editor   Alison Donovan
Publisher   Mary Ling
Art Director   Jane Bull

First published in Great Britain in 2013
by Dorling Kindersley Ltd
80 Strand, London WC2R ORL

A Penguin Company

2 4 6 8 10 9 7 5 3 1

001-187261-Feb/2013

A CIP catalogue record for this book is
available from the British Library.

ISBN 978-1-4093-8298-0

Printed and bound by
South China Co. Ltd China.

Discover more at **www.dk.com**

Contents

Steps 1–10 to preparing your plot

Simon Akeroyd was brought up in a family of professional cooks, but discovered from an early age that he preferred growing food to cooking it. He has written for numerous gardening magazines, including the monthly Allotment Gardener pages for *Grow Your Own* magazine. He was previously a Garden Manager for the Royal Horticultural Society, and has worked at both RHS Wisley and RHS Harlow Carr. He also worked for the BBC as a horticultural researcher and producer. He has an allotment in Surrey and is a keen beekeeper. His previous books include *Shrubs and Small Trees, Lawns and Ground Cover, The RHS Allotment Handbook,* and *Grow Your Own Fruit.*

Introduction

The popularity of allotments has increased enormously over the last few years, which is no surprise. Many of us live hectic desk-bound lifestyles and eat supermarket produce. We crave open spaces and home-grown fruit and vegetables – not to mention a little exercise. Working an allotment answers all these needs. Give it a try and you'll never look back.

Reaping the benefits

Growing your own food gets you outdoors and into the fresh air but it also brings many other benefits and rewards.

◆ **ALLOTMENT GARDENERS** eat more healthily than many. Having grown the recommended five-a-day portions of fruit and vegetables, they will be loath to let them go to waste.

◆ **WORKING ON** the allotment provides a fantastic outdoor workout; your muscles will ache but only in a good way.

◆ **RELAX YOUR MIND** while you garden. Leave your worries behind as you concentrate on your plants.

◆ **YOUR GARDENING** expertise will increase along with the range of fruits and vegetables you grow.

◆ **ENJOY SAVING MONEY** while you work. You are bound to appreciate harvesting tasty, fresh produce for the cost of only a few packets of seeds.

Tools

Every gardener needs decent tools to do a decent job. Don't rush to the nearest garden centre though; you can often buy second-hand tools via ads in your local paper or at car boot sales. Choose tools that suit your height and build, and be sure they feel comfortable and balanced to hold. Look after them well and clean them after use, then they will last a lifetime. The list of basic tools to get you started includes:

- a spade
- a fork
- a landscape rake
- a dibber
- a garden line or string
- a trowel
- a hand fork
- a long-handled cultivator
- dutch and draw hoes
- a watering can
- a wheelbarrow
- edging shears
- a mower (for grass paths)

Having the right tools for the job makes work on the allotment considerably easier.

Old to new

Allotments pass from tenant to tenant. Hopefully, when you take on your allotment there will be elements on it that you would be wise to retain. Old fruit bushes and trees can be revived; dilapidated raised beds and overgrown paths can be restored. Think renovation not demolition.

Established plants will prove a blessing when you are just starting out.

Wooden pallets dumped on the plot can be transformed into a compost bin.

Patio slabs left lying around can be used for paths or even seating areas.

Making friends

Whether you are retired, want to grow enough to feed your family or just love feeling the earth between your fingers, allotment life can be truly fulfilling. You may already be a keen gardener but if you are a gregarious sort of person, a bonus of having an allotment is meeting new people and making new friends while you work. Taking on a plot attracts people from all walks of life and all age groups, and most allotment societies organize regular events and activities so that members can socialize together as well as garden alongside one another. A further plus is that many allotment gardeners are only too pleased to offer help and advice, some of which will have come from their years of experience. It is like having your very own panel of gardening experts.

Gardening is a great way of spending quality time with the family. Not only do children enjoy gardening, but it gets them away from computers and TV screens and out in the fresh air.

Bring a flask to the plot and enjoy a well-earned break with your fellow gardeners.

PLOT ETIQUETTE

- Try to meet your neighbours and introduce yourself.
- Keep the paths that surround your plot clear.
- Don't allow weeds from your plot to go to seed and spread.
- Don't erect things or do any planting that will cast shade on other plots.
- Take care if using chemicals.

Plot sizes

Allotments are parcels of land that are rented out at nominal rents. Plots were traditionally quite large, with a size of 25m x 10m (80ft x 30ft) being typical. These days, sizes vary enormously and there are no hard-and-fast rules. If you are just starting out, it is better to start small; a full-size plot can be daunting and will often involve considerably more maintenance than you were expecting. Since demand has outstripped supply in many areas, sometimes only half-plots are available. If you don't feel confident taking on a plot on your own, consider sharing one with a friend.

Reuse and recycle

When you take on an allotment you will quickly discover how to become a master – or mistress – of recycling. You won't let anything go to waste.

◆ **HANG OLD CDS** among your crops and they will act as bird scarers; empty toilet-roll tubes miraculously become plant pots; and old tyres filled with soil prove perfect for growing potatoes.

◆ **RE-USE PLASTIC POTS** and trays; you can never have enough at seed-sowing time.

◆ **PLASTIC BOTTLES** make cloches for protecting young seedlings. Pushed into the soil and filled with water, they become handy reservoirs.

About this book

The first three chapters of this book show the progression of a new plot, from planning and preparation, to the well-earned harvest. These chapters also feature step-by-step projects, built and photographed on a real allotment, to show what can be achieved in the first year. The final chapter explains how to troubleshoot common problems, while a useful glossary will help you understand unfamiliar gardening terminology.

Real allotment Watch the development of a real plot over a year.

Practical help Advice panels help get the best from even difficult sites.

10 steps to preparing your plot Starting with a new plot, follow the steps in sequence to ensure success. Take time to assess and plan your site properly before starting work, to avoid problems later on.

Raised beds Follow the step-by-step guide to make your own.

Materials needed Use these guides as a shopping list, so you have everything you need at every stage.

Projects You don't have to be an expert at DIY to follow these straightforward guides to making features for your plot. All projects involve simple tools and materials that are widely available.

Chapter 1:
Preparing the plot

This chapter explains the 10 essential steps required to bring a new allotment to life. Starting with assessing the site to decide what crops will grow best, it shows how to prepare the soil, sow seeds under cover or outside, then illustrates all the tasks and techniques necessary for a bumper crop. The chapter also features simple step-by-step projects to help make the most of the site. These include laying paths and making raised beds, erecting rabbit-proof fencing, and making a cold frame. This chapter also reminds you to enjoy your plot, and to take time to make it your own.

Additional info boxes These provide useful tips to make tasks easier, or suggest other options.

Chapters 2 & 3:
Growing vegetables & fruit

These chapters provide in-depth growing instructions to over 70 different fruits, vegetables, and herbs. Starting with sowing seeds or planting new plants, the instructions cover every stage of each crop's development, explaining what to do, when, and how. There are also step-by-step projects, showing how to build features that make growing your crops easier and more successful.

Storing & Using

After the excitement of growing your food comes the joy of eating it. Every grower is thrilled to have a bumper crop but what to do when you are faced with a glut?

Storing Discover how best to store your crops so that they can be enjoyed in perfect condition.

Freezing You can extend the life of much of your produce by freezing it; discover how to do it and how long you can store it for.

Cooking There are lots of exciting recipe ideas to help you make the most of your crops.

Preserving Delicious jams, preserves, and chutneys can be made from gluts of fruit and veg.

Info boxes Refer to the panels for timely tips and advice.

Veg: Growing and storing The crops in chapter two are organized according to type, such as "leafy crops", so they are easy to find. Crop type relates to the part of the vegetable that is commonly eaten, whether that's the leaves, roots, stems, flowers, or pods.

Fruit: Growing & storing The fruit crops featured in chapter three are either soft fruits, such as strawberries and raspberries, or tree and vine fruits, such as apples and grapes.

Chapter 4: Help

This final chapter shows how to prevent or resolve many of the common problems that can occur on allotments. Illustrated galleries help to identify pests, diseases, and weeds, and give advice on how to treat them. There is also practical advice on pruning fruit trees and bushes to keep them healthy, and a guide to propagating your own plants when you need to increase your stocks.

steps 1-10

to preparing your plot

step 1

assessing your site

an inherited site • allotment
checklist • carrying out
renovations
• an overgrown site
• sunny & shady sites

Assessing your site

Your first visit to a potential new allotment site may be daunting, particularly if it has become very overgrown. But don't despair – armed with a strimmer, spade and garden fork, you can transform it into a thriving vegetable plot over the next few months.

Potatoes
Planted by the previous tenant, these potatoes are a welcome find and will definitely stay to provide the first harvest of the year.

Path from reclaimed slabs
The existing slabs can remain in place for now as they make a sturdy path and will keep emerging weeds at bay.

Allotment checklist

When you are first looking round a plot, consider the following:
◆ Are the neighbouring plots neat and tidy? (You don't want weeds straying onto your plot.)
◆ What is the access like?
◆ Is there a water supply nearby?
◆ Are there fruit trees, vegetable plants and other items such as cold frames that can be salvaged?
◆ Is there a regular rubbish collection?

"Keep a lookout for anything that can be **recycled**"

Raspberries These canes are on the edge of the plot and can remain as a useful screen.

Area to renovate The area in the centre of the plot will make a good starting point, enabling it to be expanded later in the year. Once the area has been cleared of debris, it can be measured up and some new raised beds made.

Strawberry patch These can stay in place for now as they will suppress weeds and hopefully supply a good crop of berries in summer. Next year, the younger plants can be lifted and planted in a new bed.

Raised beds Pieces of timber can be recycled to edge the vegetable beds.

Logs It may be possible to use these to create the legs for a bench.

Area to renovate

Once the site has been cleared, choose an area to cultivate first. By starting in a small way, growing your own food will seem less daunting than if you try to cultivate the entire plot all at once. The owner of this plot (left) has decided to cultivate the area in the centre first because it has nothing worth keeping and so can be cleared completely, whereas other areas of the plot have fruit trees and other plants. The previous occupant has left some really useful material behind, including a sleeper, which will make a great bench, and some old pieces of timber from which raised beds can be constructed.

Completely overgrown site

Your first task is to blitz the weeds so you can see the bare bones of your site. Wear gloves and protective clothing as there could be broken glass, wasps' nests, bottles of chemicals and other hazardous items lurking in the brambles. Start by either strimming or applying a systemic weedkiller to eradicate the worst of the weeds. Look out for plants to save, and useful material such as wood. Sometimes the council will help with initial clearance.

Keep anything useful Keep a lookout for anything that can be recycled, such as timber for raised beds or pallets for making compost bins.

Salvage Old raised beds may be salvageable.

Rejuvenate Fruit trees and bushes can be restored by pruning.

Different types of site

Before planning your plot, first assess your site to determine which areas are sunny or shaded and for how long during the day, as this will affect the crops you can grow. Similarly, if your plot is at the bottom of a slope it may sit in a frost pocket, so you will need to grow hardier crops, or plant out only once the frosts have passed. Plots at the top of slopes can be cold and windy, which may rule out tall or tender crops.

SITE CHECKLIST

- Which direction does it face?
- Is it sunny for most of the day?
- Is it shady for most of the day?
- Is it exposed or sheltered?
- Does the ground slope?
- Are there potential frost pockets?
- Is there easy access to a water tap?

Orientation Use a compass to work out the direction your plot faces. South-facing sites are warm, north-facing are cool.

A clean slate Clearing an existing plot enables you to plan your crops to best suit the site and soil conditions.

If you have a sunny site

Sunny sites provide the best growing conditions, warming up quickly in spring and allowing the longest growing season. If you also have a wall or fence to provide shelter, fruit and fruiting vegetables, such as peppers, tomatoes, aubergines, cucumbers, and squashes, will do well, and root and salad crops will also flourish. The downside is that the soil will dry out quickly and you may need to water your crops more often, even daily during hot weather. Add well-rotted organic matter to the soil to help retain moisture, and mulch around crops regularly.

Aspect

The aspect, or direction, your plot faces plays a vital role in how well your crops grow. It not only determines how sunny or shaded the plot is, and for how long during the day, but also affects the direct the wind blows from, and even how much rain it receives. While you can reduce the effects of aspects by removing shade-casting obstacles or by installing windbreaks, it is best to grow according to the conditions.

If you have a shady site

Shady sites are more limiting than sunny plots because most fruit and vegetables require some sun. They are also colder with a shorter growing season, which means sun-loving crops, such as tomatoes and aubergines, may struggle. Try to reduce the amount of shade by pruning overhanging trees, or move or remove obstacles that are casting shade. Opt for crops that don't mind some shade, such as potatoes, lettuces and salad leaves, spinach, radishes, and Jerusalem artichokes. If you have sunnier areas on the plot, use these for crops that need brighter conditions.

If you have an exposed or hilly site

Plots on hills are often exposed and windy, although are less prone to frosts than those in valleys. To increase your choice of crops, and to improve their success rates, install a windbreak, such as a hedge, or an open-weave fence that allows some wind to pass through. Tall crops, such as sweetcorn and fruit trees, may still suffer wind damage, so plant low-growers instead, such as root crops, salad leaves, and hardy fruits, like strawberries and raspberries. Wind also dries the soil very quickly, so make sure you install an efficient watering system.

If you have a site in a frost pocket

Frost pockets commonly occur at the base of hills, in valleys, and on north-facing slopes, or simply where the cold air can't escape due to walls, fences, or dense hedges. Frosts can severely damage plants, particularly young seedlings and emerging spring blossom. They can also destroy crops in autumn if they haven't been harvested soon enough. Protect plants by covering them with fleece and cloches. Delay planting outside until all threat of frosts has passed, and harden them off fully. Keeping the net roofs on fruit cages can raise the temperature at night by a few degrees.

South-facing plot This is an ideal aspect for sun-loving crops, as the plot will not be shaded by neighbouring trees, sheds, or hedges. The plot will be warm and bright.

West-facing plot This allotment will be bathed in sunshine for most of the day, except for early in the morning, when the sun will be rising from behind the hedge.

North-facing plot This plot could be shady if the hedge isn't kept low, as it will cast shade over the south side of the plot at midday. The shed will also cast shade.

East-facing plot The west side of this plot will be in shade, so crops here won't benefit from the warm evening sun. The shed would be better sited at the north end.

step 2

preparing your soil

know your soil •
what's in your soil • the acid
test • improving your soil •
clearing the weeds
• fertilizers • double digging

sandy soil

clay soil

silty soil

chalky soil

step 2 Know your soil

Is your soil dry and dusty, sticky and wet, or a crumbly mix of the two? Whatever your soil type, there are plenty of crops that will thrive on it, as some like free-draining sand, while others prefer nutrient-rich clay. There are also easy ways of improving soil to create the perfect "loam" that most crops love.

What's in your soil?

The type of soil you have in your garden or on your allotment is determined by the ground rock below it, and by the amount of organic matter, such as decayed plants and animal manure, that it contains. Most soils are either rich in sand or clay, while a few near coastal sites may be silty and those over limestone rock are thin and chalky. The best soils, known as "loams", contain a mixture of clay and sand, and are easy to work, retain water and nutrients, and drain well. Although few of us are lucky enough to have loam, there are ways to improve all soils, whatever their composition.

◆ **TO DETERMINE YOUR** soil type, take a small sample in your hands and press it between your fingers. Clay soil will form a ball when rolled, while sandy soil feels gritty and falls apart when you try to roll it. Silty soil feels a little like clay, but has a more silky texture. If you have chalky soil, you will see the white chalky deposits running through it and it will dry out quickly, like sand.

"Knowing your soil type will help you make the most of it"

Clay soil This is sticky and wet to the touch, and forms a ball when rolled between the hands.

Sandy soil This feels gritty and damp; it will simply fall apart if you try to roll it into a ball.

Silty soil This behaves more like clay, but it feels silky. It will also form a ball when rolled.

alkaline

acid

THE ACID TEST As well as assessing your soil for its sand or clay content, you should also find out its pH value, which is a measure of its acidity or alkalinity. You can do this very easily with a pH kit. Simply add a small sample of soil to the liquid provided and the resulting colour will show the acid content of your soil. Most crops grow well in neutral to slightly alkaline soil, but you need acid conditions to grow crops such as blueberries. If your soil is alkaline, simply grow acid-lovers in containers of ericaceous (acid) potting compost.

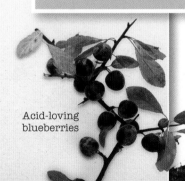

Acid-loving blueberries

Improving your soil

Successful fruit and vegetable growing is all about preparation.
Before you sow a single seed, there is a lot of work to do. Once
the soil has been cleared of weeds, it must be thoroughly dug
over and levelled. If the soil is poor, it will need improving
with organic matter before finally reducing the soil down to
a fine tilth, or nice crumbly consistency. Having done all this,
you will be ready to sow your first seeds.

Pull out weeds Take care not to snap the roots when levering out perennial roots with a fork, or the weeds will quickly grow again.

Remove large objects first

Before you put your garden
fork into the soil, start by
clearing the surface first,
removing all rubbish, broken
glass and large stones or
bricks. Consider hiring a skip
if there is a large amount of
material to clear.

Clear the weeds

It is well worth spending time
thoroughly clearing the site of
weeds right from the start. Once
seeds are sown and crops are planted, it becomes considerably
harder to eradicate them from the plot. Use a fork to dig them
out, as a spade can slice through perennial roots, encouraging them
to multiply. Make sure you fork over the entire bed because weeds
will spread very quickly if they aren't dealt with from the word go.

Be thorough
Perennial weeds such
as ground elder, couch
grass and dandelions
will continue to grow
if just a tiny piece of
root is left in the
ground. Dig deeply,
as plants such as
bindweed can have
roots that extend as
deep as 60cm (24in)
into the soil.

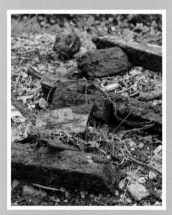

Keep or discard
Have a careful look
through the rubbish.
Consider whether
some of the material
could be recycled.
Rubber tyres can make
great containers for
potatoes, while bricks
or slabs could be used
to make paths.

"Weeds will spread if they aren't eradicated at the start"

Dig over and level the site

Once the site has been cleared of weeds, use a spade to dig it over. Choose a spade that feels comfortable for you, is light and of a suitable length. Avoid lifting too much soil on your spade each time you dig as it can damage your back. The soil should ideally be dug down to a depth of around 45cm (18in), ensuring that any compacted soil, or "pans", are broken up in the process.

Digging technique Keep your knees bent and your back as straight as possible to avoid injury.

Ready for improvement After removing weeds, the beds can be dug over using a spade. This loosens the soil and improves the consistency.

Double digging (see p.24) The bed should be dug over to twice the depth of the spade head. Fill the bottom 20cm (8in) with organic matter.

Levelling Once the soil has been dug over, it should be roughly levelled using a landscape rake or the back of a spade.

Fertilizers

The soil of your plot will probably need improving to grow crops successfully. Adding organic matter to the soil after double digging will encourage the roots to penetrate deeply and find nutrients and water. However, young seedlings and shallow-rooting plants will need their nourishment to be closer to the surface. There is a wide range of materials that can be added to the soil and lightly dug into it afterwards.

Farmyard material Add lots of organic matter to the surface. This helps to suppress weeds and improve the growing potential.

Compost Well-rotted garden compost will help to retain moisture around young seedlings and will be full of nutrients.

Chemical General-purpose fertilizers will provide young plants with a much-needed boost in the early stages of growth.

Project
Double digging

Double digging is usually carried out if the ground has not been previously cultivated or if drainage and soil structure need to be improved. It is worth the hard work and will result in better soil quality.

step **2**

step **3**

Move the soil from the first trench to just beyond the end of the plot. Use it to fill in the final trench.

step **1**

MATERIALS & TOOLS

- organic matter, manure or compost
- spade, fork, rake, bucket

1 Begin by digging a trench at one end of the bed to the depth of your spade and approximately twice as wide. Keep the width and depth consistent as you dig, and try to keep the sides as neat as possible. Remove any weeds and large stones you find.

2 Put the excavated soil from this trench into a large bucket or a wheelbarrow. This will be used to fill in the final trench at the end of the bed.

3 Dig and loosen the soil in the base of the first trench to another spade's depth, breaking up any big, hard lumps, and removing any stones or debris.

4 Now add well-rotted manure or compost to the bottom of the trench and lightly fork it in.

5 Dig the second trench directly adjacent to the first, and to the same dimensions. Use the soil dug out to fill in the first trench. Once again, remove any weeds, stones, or other debris as you go.

6 Similarly, use soil from the third trench to fill the second, once organic matter has been forked in. Repeat this process all the way down the plot. Finally, use the soil set aside from the first trench to fill in the top layer of the last.

step 4

Dig the organic matter into the loosened soil at the base of the trench, so it is well distributed.

Keep the excavated trenches the same size, so the spoil from one is enough to fill the previous.

Why double dig?

For your plot to support healthy, vigorous crops, it needs to be well drained and aerated. Incorporating well-rotted organic matter will feed your crops and also improve soil structure. This technique is so-named because each trench is dug twice; once to remove the top layer and any weeds, and a second time to loosen and aerate the sub-layer, and to introduce organic matter.

Move trench 1 soil to the end

step 5

The soil deposited in the first trench will sit higher than it was originally, but will eventually settle.

Dig over the base of the last trench in the same way as previous ones, and add manure or compost.

The soil saved from the first trench, here stored on the path, can now be used to fill in the final trench.

step 6

All that remains is to rake over the plot until a fine tilth is achieved, ready for sowing or planting. Avoid walking on the newly dug plot at first, as the soil will become compacted.

step 3

creating your space

beds & borders • plan your space
• choosing paths • materials
for paths • marking out the
area • prepare the edges
• prepare the surface
• raised beds

step 3

Beds & borders

Creating the beds and borders on your plot is an exciting stage in the development of your allotment design. There are a number of practical considerations to take into account, but you can also allow the creative side of your brain to have a say and consider different shapes or use recycled, quirky materials to give it a personal touch.

Position and types of beds

Deciding where the beds are going to be placed is key to the overall design of the plot. The most popular and simplest solution is to create beds directly into the soil. Access is important, so make sure you leave enough room between the beds to get your wheelbarrow up and down.

◆ **RAISED BEDS** are the perfect solution to gardening on poor soil. Once built and filled with good-quality compost, the benefits are enormous. There is no more backbreaking weeding, while planting and harvesting are made much easier. The extra height means the soil is well-drained and it warms up more quickly in the spring. Another benefit is that the crops will ripen more quickly.

Beds size guide

The size of the beds is a matter of personal preference. However, it is important to be able to reach the middle of a bed without walking on the soil and compacting it, so it's sensible to restrict the width to about 1m (3ft). You can be more flexible about length, but remember you can fit in more crops if you have fewer paths.

- Beds should be narrow enough to reach into the middle.
- Paths should be wide enough to accommodate a wheelbarrow.

A good size These beds allow room for a range of crops, yet are narrow enough to work on without walking on the soil.

Concrete slabs These large, heavy blocks make a very robust structure for edging the beds. Thanks to their weight, they may not need digging into the soil.

Log rolls Wood is a popular material for edging a bed. Make sure that the timber is suitable for outdoor use or it will quickly rot. Use pegs to secure it in place.

Victorian edging stones For a more formal effect in the vegetable beds, use these attractive Victorian stones. Original ones are quite easy to obtain.

"Get your plans and design ideas down on paper"

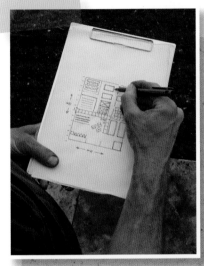

Draw a plan Sketching out a plan of your plot is a very useful exercise that will help you to prioritize what you want to include.

Plan your space

Get your plans and design ideas down on paper. This is best done on site so that you can get a better feel for the plot. You will probably make several drafts before you decide on what will work best for the space you have available. Don't worry about specific planting at this stage; this is just a rough sketch to determine the underlying structure of the plot. Think about where you want to create fruit and vegetable beds, where you want paths, a shed, a cold frame, compost bin, onion rack and perhaps a seating or barbecue area. If you have a large plot, you may want to consider including a sandpit, children's toy area, or even a swing or slide.

Ideas for recycled raised beds

Almost any container or box can be used on the allotment as a raised bed. Just ensure that the material is durable, weatherproof and has adequate drainage to prevent plant roots from rotting.

Old sink Not only does this make a beautiful feature, but the plughole also makes the perfect drainage hole.

Drainage pipes These terracotta pipes are good and deep – ideal for growing vegetables with long roots.

Tyres These are perfect for growing sweet peas. They also work for potatoes; stack more tyres on top as they grow.

Metal edging Beds edged in metal will give your allotment an urban feel. Be aware, though, that they heat up in the sun, which can burn plant roots.

Wooden planks These are quick and easy to install and will do the job of keeping the compost in place, but they may not last as long as other types of edging.

Choosing your paths

Once the beds have been constructed, you can start to consider the layout and material for the paths. They need to be as functional as possible as this will enable you to work efficiently. Unlike garden paths, paths on the allotment do not need to take much weight and probably won't require cement or lots of hardcore as a base. This means they can usually be made using limited DIY or landscaping skills.

Bricks These are one of the most durable materials for paths. They don't necessarily need cementing together, as long as they are bedded firmly into the soil.

Materials to use

There is a wide variety of different materials that can be used to make paths, all of which can be quite costly to buy, so first take a look around to see what material can be recycled. Check local skips to see if landscaping companies are throwing out old paving slabs, or see if you can obtain materials free via your local Freecycle website. Essentially, a path can be made of anything, including ornamental bark chip, bricks or even carpet; the choice is yours.

◆ **GRASS PATHS** are probably the cheapest to make if you can't find anything to recycle. Not only do they provide a soft, durable and natural surface, but the seed is also very cheap.

Carpet tiles These make an attractive and surprisingly hard-wearing path, although they can be prone to rot after prolonged periods of cold, wet weather.

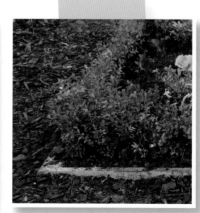

Bark chips Using a natural material such as this popular mulch gives a path a lovely finish, but it needs to be edged to avoid the bark spilling onto the beds.

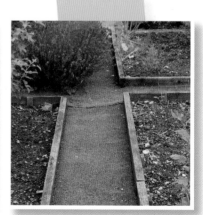

Artificial turf If you like the look of grass paths, but don't want to spend time mowing and edging them, then artificial turf could be the answer, but it is not a cheap option.

Use your plan to mark out the area Plot out where the paths are to go. They provide your route for moving around the plot, so they need to be practical, functional and ideally take you straight from A to B.

Edging the paths

Hard landscaped paths should be finished with an edge to retain their structure and prevent loose material such as bark chips and gravel from spilling onto the beds. Grass paths don't require an edge, but will look much smarter if the sides are regularly clipped with edging shears and given definition each season with the edge of a spade.

String and bamboo canes Use these to mark out where you want to create your paths. Take into account the areas where you are most frequently going to walk, which will include accessing water butts and compost heaps.

Bamboo canes Insert these at the corners of paths and intersections; push them in far enough to take the strain of the string and ensure they are straight. Once they are in place, wind the string around them to give an outline of paths and beds.

Mark the perimeter Once the paths have been marked out, the soil should be levelled and all humps and bumps flattened out. The surface should be lightly trodden down and compacted to prevent the path sinking at a later date.

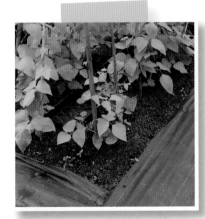

Weed-supressing membrane Not the most attractive of materials, but it will suppress weeds and create a smooth surface. It looks better if covered with bark chip.

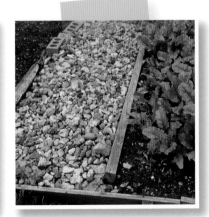

Gravel This material needs to be laid on a weed-supressing membrane and edged or it will eventually disappear into the soil. It is not easy to push a wheelbarrow on.

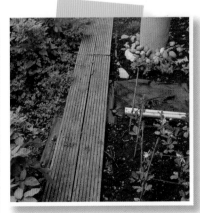

Decking boards Be careful not to slip on these boards as they can be treacherous when wet. Choose boards with grooves cut into them; alternatively, saw your own.

Project Part 1
Paths: Mark out the area

To get the best use out of your allotment, the paths and access routes should be well planned to make sure you can easily reach all areas of your plot. The most heavily used routes will benefit from a properly constructed path which, as well as being practical, will improve the look of the whole area.

step **2**

Every corner joint and intersection should have a stake to support it.

Make the frames

This allotment (see right) has been set out with raised beds in the middle, with their frames also forming the edges to some of the paths. The bed frames and path edges are made in the same way using planks and stakes – assemble them on a workbench or any level area. Cut the timber sides to length and join them at the corners with screws, using simple butt joints (see below). Use only pressure-treated timber, which resists decay, to prolong the life of your paths and beds.

step **1**

Path stakes only need to protrude slightly higher than the edge, and can be trimmed later. Bed stakes that support nets should be longer.

Ensure bed corners are at right angles using a builder's square. Attach timber diagonals to support and hold the frames together.

Screw the joints Holding both sides of the bed frame or path edge steady, screw the joints together. You may find it easier to drill small pilot holes for the screws.

1 Mark out the plot using canes and string as a guide, and temporarily place the bed frames in position. It's likely that they will not sit very squarely to begin with, so it may be necessary to level the soil surface using a rake or spade.

2 Once the beds and the path edges are in place, work out how many stakes are needed – one for each corner, and one every 1.5m (5ft) along the sides – and lay them out.

step 3

Pointed stakes

The stakes should be long enough to support the full height of the planks, plus a further 20cm (8in), which is driven into the soil. Before the stakes are hammered into the ground it is useful to cut one end into a point to make the task easier.

Use a wooden or metal stake to form pilot holes. This will make it easier to drive in the stakes squarely. It will also help to lever buried stones out of the way.

The top of the path edging should be a little higher than the soil level to prevent earth falling onto the path.

Drive the stakes in as squarely as possible. Ideally, their tops should be level with the top of the timber they are supporting; they can be tapped in further or trimmed as required.

3 Once you are satisfied with the layout of the paths and beds, begin to drive in the prepared stakes for the path edges.

4 Each stake should be driven into the ground to a depth of at least 20cm (8in), although this will need to be increased if the ground is soft and unsupportive.

5 With the beds still temporarily in place, line up the path edges against their stakes to finalize their positions. Some stakes may need slight adjustment so they line up properly.

MATERIALS & TOOLS

- lengths of treated board, timber stakes, screws, string line, bamboo canes
- lump hammer, straight metal bar, screwdriver, workbench, clamps, builder's square, spade, rake

Project Part 2
Paths: Prepare the edges

Once the planning and initial preparation of the path edges is done, the area will begin to take shape. The stakes have been driven in, and the paths and beds have been set out. If your plot is on level ground, levelling and positioning of the edges is easy, but will be more time consuming if the site slopes.

The existing path between this allotment and the one next to it was level, so was used as the starting point. The first path edge was placed parallel to it, and at a similar height.

Lie of the land

This particular site slopes gently and consistently from north to south. As a result, while some of the edges sit quite level, those at right angles to them will have to follow the existing ground level. As long as you bed the edges in well, the paths will be sturdy and practical.

To save timber, you can join sections that are not long enough. An extra stake can be driven in at the joint, or use an offcut to overlap both ends and screw together, as shown here.

step 1

If there are paths that lead off the main path, remember to leave corresponding gaps in the edging. This will be easier than cutting them out later.

You may find that the timber available is usually no more than 5 metres (15ft) long. As most allotments are longer or wider than this, some joints are inevitable.

1   First choose a level section of path edging and screw the timber planks to the stakes. This can then be used as a starting point for the next section. Lay the edging against the stakes and adjust the height as necessary, comparing it to surrounding ground levels. Hold the timber edges in place temporarily with clamps, or prop them up with stones. You may need to dig out areas where the soil level is too high.

step 2

2 With most of the path edges in place, the raised beds can be temporarily laid back into position to check their levels.

3 The side paths can now be fixed, using the main path as a guideline. Line up the edges to see if any soil needs to be removed before joining them together.

Attach path edges to the stakes where they meet at corners to give a strong join.

Ensuring that you do not push the timber out of line, drive the stake in flush to the edge of the board and screw together as normal.

step 3

With the frames back in place you can now see clearly how much, if any, soil needs to be removed to ensure that they sit neatly in position.

step 4

You will rarely have spare earth on an allotment; the excess earth from the paths is being used in the raised beds, or can also be used for many other purposes.

step 5

4 With the path edges in place, you may find you require additional stakes to hold them firm, especially if the site slopes.

5 Now that the paths are formed and the bed positions marked out, you can easily see where soil must be moved to level the paths and build up the beds.

Project Part 3
Paths: Prepare the surface

Now the path edges have been fixed into position, you are nearing the final stages of the project. This next step involves preparing the surface of the paths so they are durable and easy to maintain, and installing the frames for the raised beds. Once completed, the area will be transformed into a recognizable growing space.

step 2

Membrane tips

Once the membrane has been laid, a good way to prevent weeds growing along the sides of the paths is to tuck the membrane under the path edging. If the timber sits tight to the soil, scrape some away, then tuck the fabric under.

Use stones or old bricks to hold the membrane in place while you continue to lay it.

step 1

Trim excess membrane once all the paths have been covered. Cut it using scissors or a utility knife.

1 Starting at a place where it is easy to work, lay strips of weed-proof membrane along the paths, overlapping the sides where the raised beds will be sited.

2 Work your way over the whole area, covering the paths with membrane. You may need help to lay and hold the membrane in position.

Tip chipped bark or gravel onto the membrane once whole sections of path are covered.

step 3

To ensure the raised beds are level with the path edging, lay a piece of straight timber across them. Raise and lower the edges accordingly, then screw the framework to the stakes.

When secured, the raised bed frames will conveniently hold down the weed membrane. Any diagonal support braces on the frames can now be removed.

step 4

3 Place the raised bed frames in position, tuck the membrane beneath their sides, and screw them to their stakes.

4 With all the weed membrane tucked neatly under the path and bed edging, trim off any excess material. Cover the membrane with bark or gravel, levelling and compacting it in layers.

5 The path will eventually settle and may need topping up. Apply a fresh layer of bark or gravel each year, and remove any weeds that poke through.

Remove the stones or bricks used to weigh down the membrane and rake out the bark or gravel to cover the paths. Try not to snag the membrane.

step 5

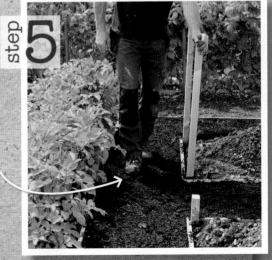

MATERIALS & TOOLS
- weed mat or membrane, chipped bark or gravel
- utility knife or scissors, wheelbarrow, rake, shovel

Tread the surface down by walking over it repeatedly. This will create a firmer, more durable finish.

...raised beds

Project Part 4
Raised beds

The final stage of the project is to finish the raised beds and fill them with soil, ready for sowing and planting. The height you choose depends on what you want to grow, and how good the underlying soil is. Make deeper beds to grow root crops and if the soil is poor; shallower beds for leaf and pod crops, and if the soil below is reasonable.

The boards that comprise the raised bed frames should not only be screwed to each other, but also to the corner stakes.

step **1**

step **2**

step **3**

1   The construction of the raised beds is the same as previously outlined (see p.32). However, depending on your growing requirements, their depth can be altered using wider or narrower edges. Scaffolding planks and decking boards are popular choices.

2   Once the frames are in place and have been securely fixed to the stakes, they can be filled with earth.

3   Rake the soil roughly level with the top of the boards, picking out larger stones and any debris, and add well-rotted organic matter before planting.

MATERIALS & TOOLS

- timber planks – recycled scaffolding planks or decking boards, timber, screws, nails
- hammer, screwdriver, shovel, rake

Simple options

One of the benefits of raised beds is that you can make them to suit your needs, which also includes keeping them simple. Beds can be made of anything that will contain soil, and don't have to be permanent. Large stones or old railway sleepers can easily be placed on the ground to form temporary beds. Raised beds can also be bought as kits, and put together on any firm, level surface.

Temporary beds Large planters grouped together provide a simple way to make a short-term raised bed. Butt them up as close as possible.

Kits There are many types of raised bed kits to choose, made of concrete (above), wood, woven panels, and plastic. Most just simply lock together.

This raised bed has long stakes at the corners, which enables the produce grown in it to be easily covered with netting.

A typical raised bed is around 15cm (6in) deep, but can be deeper. The supporting stakes have been cut level with the edging boards.

A ground-level bed has a useful wooden edge to provide a barrier between the soil and surrounding path, serving to contain the plants and soil within.

step 4

protecting crops

protection from wind, frost, & pests • rabbit-proof fencing • greenhouses & cold frames • make a cold frame • cloches

step 4 Protection from wind, frost, & pests

The delight of growing your own food can sometimes be diminished by the discovery that your crops have been destroyed. Pests such as birds and slugs are opportunists and will feast on your vegetables unless you get there first, while wind can reduce foliage to ribbons unless you have provided protection.

Cage the plot The simplest solution to protecting crops from birds is to net the whole plot.

Screening tips

Air circulation among your crops is healthy; it helps to prevent a build-up of pests and diseases, so it is better if a windbreak is permeable. Avoid screening with walls and fences but instead plant hedges or erect trellis.

Trellis This will protect your plants from harsh winds while still allowing the air to circulate.

Low screening This will protect seedlings but the wind will pass over the top and may damage taller crops.

Windbreaks

Allotments usually nestle cheek by jowl with one another. This means that they are often afforded some protection from the wind. However, if they are on a slope or at the edge of the site, then crops can easily be damaged and even blown over. There are many ways to shelter your crops from strong winds and you may not even need to screen the whole plot but just the edge that faces the prevailing wind.

Choose a windbreak that suits the height of your crops

Netting to protect against birds & insects

Keep a lookout for pests and try to predict their feeding habits. Sadly, they are often only noticed when it is too late and they have already inflicted irreparable damage. Birds are the worst offenders, attacking ripe fruit and emerging vegetable shoots and foliage. Cages offer the best protection and you can buy bespoke cages to suit your individual requirements. However, it is just as easy to make your own cages by lashing bamboo canes together and draping the requisite type of netting over the whole structure.

Squirrels Robust cages are needed to protect crops against squirrels as their sharp teeth and claws easily rip through netting.

Cabbage white butterfly Members of the cabbage family should be covered with fine-mesh netting to keep this pest at bay.

Birds Cover leafy crops with netting to prevent birds from ripping the lush foliage. This is the only certain way to protect vulnerable plants.

Rabbits (see Project, pp.44–47) Erect rabbit or chicken fencing around the plot and dig it down into the soil to keep rabbits out.

"Air circulation is healthy so windbreaks should be permeable"

Slugs & snails

These can strip seedlings of their foliage in hours. Surround plants with gravel, sand, bran or copper as slugs and snails don't like to crawl on these materials. Plastic containers in the soil and filled with beer will attract them. Snails fall into the trap and can't escape.

Plastic collars

Copper barriers

Brassica collar

Project Part 1
Rabbit-proof fencing

Rabbits graze a wide variety of plants, and can cause a considerable amount of damage in vegetable and fruit gardens, usually overnight. If your plot is in an area known to have rabbits present, it is best to take preventative measures and install a rabbit-proof fence to protect your valuable produce.

step 3

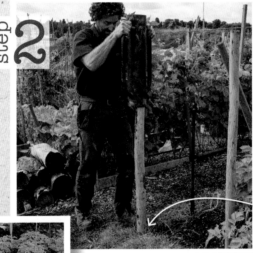

Position the four corner posts first. Once these have been driven in, a string line can be pulled taut between them to act as a guide for the remaining posts. This will ensure that they are in line, which will make attaching the wire far easier, as well as looking neater.

step 2

Leave enough space for the garden gate to be fitted; it will need approximately 1cm (½in) extra on each side so that it can open and close freely.

The posts should go in to a depth of around 30cm (12in) but this is dependent upon how soft the ground is.

step 1

1 First ensure that the perimeter of the allotment is free of obstacles, then make a pilot hole at each corner using a metal bar or thin stake, 30cm (12in) deep, and slightly less than the thickness of the fence posts.

2 Drive the corner posts into the pilot holes, checking they are level. Either use a sledgehammer, which may splinter the tops, or hire a "post knocker" (see above), which won't, and will drive them in straighter.

3 Run a string line between the four corner posts as a guide, and position more posts along the length, spaced 1.8m (6ft) apart. Make a pilot hole for each one, as before.

step 4

Supporting posts

Corner posts and gate posts need to be especially rigid, as they will be taking the strain of the fencing wire when it is pulled taut, plus the weight of the gate. This can be achieved by using wider posts here, or by attaching diagonal braces (see p.196).

step 5

Digging the trench allows you to bury the fencing wire into the soil, preventing rabbits digging under it.

Wearing thick gloves, roll out the wire up to and beyond the next corner post, keeping it as taut as possible. Fold out the lower 15cm (6in) to line the base of the trench.

4 Drive all the posts in firmly, so they move very little when pushed. Now dig a trench around the entire perimeter, 15cm (6in) wide and deep.

5 At the top of one corner post, nail or staple the fencing wire 1m (3ft) above ground level, with 30cm (12in) at the bottom to line the trench.

6 Using fencing pliers, tension the wire fencing as much as possible, or ask an assistant to pull it tight by hand. Nail or staple the fencing wire onto the next corner post, repeating this on all sides.

step 6

MATERIALS & TOOLS

- round or half-round posts 1.5m (5ft) long, galvanized chicken or rabbit fencing 1.3m (4½ft) high – the maximum mesh size should be 2½cm (1in) – fencing nails, 10cm (4in) galvanized clout nails, treated boards for top rail, screws
- claw hammer or fencing pliers, sledgehammer or post knocker, metal bar or wooden stake, hand saw, screwdriver, spirit level

On the final post, cut the wire, fold the ends in, and nail it neatly onto the post to prevent snagging yourself on any sharp loose ends.

...part two

Project Part 2
Rabbit-proof fencing

With the fencing wire neatly nailed into position, the fence can now be made rabbit-proof. Installing a top rail will prevent the wire sagging between the posts, and also gives a neater finish. A close-fitting gate will make the allotment easily accessible, but not to rabbits.

step 9

MATERIALS & TOOLS

- reclaimed gate, latch, gate hinges
- tools as previous page

Compact the soil thoroughly at the base of the posts. Once complete, gently rake the surface to a level finish.

step 8

Clamp the top rail in place temporarily before securing with screws at least 5cm (2in) long. The joints between the top rails should meet at a post.

Scrape the excavated soil into the trench and rake it level. Ensure the wire fencing is well buried.

step 7

7   Use the previously excavated soil to fill in the trench and cover the bottom of the fence wire.

8   Once the trench has been filled and levelled, it will need to be compacted firmly. Tread the soil down with your heel, all the way around.

9   Mark the posts at around 1m (3ft) above ground level using a string line as a guide, and line up the top rail. The fencing wire should come to about halfway up this rail, where it can be nailed in.

step 10

Cut the posts to the same height above the top rail to give a neater finish, although it is not essential.

step 11

Fix the gate hinges in position. Use only one or two screws at first, to see whether the gate opens and closes properly, before driving in the rest of the screws.

Diagonal braces help to support the gate posts, and can also be used to strengthen the corners.

10 Pull the fencing wire upward so it is taut, and nail or tack it to the inside of the top rail. Do this all the way around the fence before trimming the post tops.

11 Using offcuts of timber as wedges, hold the gate in place, allowing as little space as possible at the bottom, while still being able to open and close it easily. The space at the sides should be equal. Mark the position of the hinges and drill pilot holes slightly smaller than the diameter of the screws being used.

Rabbits are unable to scale the fence and the wire buried below ground level will deter them from burrowing underneath. The fence also creates a neat appearance.

Greenhouses & cold frames

A greenhouse is a useful addition to any vegetable plot, allowing you to give crops a head start, grow tender varieties, and extend the growing season. Cold frames also allow crops to be started earlier and are ideal for hardening off seedlings before planting them in the ground outside.

Greenhouses

Greenhouses come in a range of sizes and materials, and can be adapted to growing a wide range of crops, even all year. New greenhouses can be expensive but it is often possible to buy them locally secondhand, so check your local papers.

◆ **THE BENEFITS** of having a greenhouse are huge. They provide the perfect growing conditions to raise seedlings, enable you to grow a wide range of heat-loving crops, such as aubergines and chillies, and also double-up as a potting shed, allowing you to work even if the weather is bad.

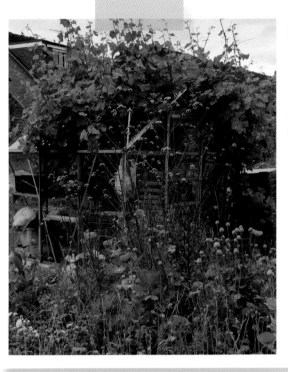

Summer shade This grapevine provides much-needed shade during summer, preventing the plants inside being scorched or over-heating. Shade netting or shade paint can also be used.

Provide perfect growing conditions

Collect rainwater from the roof

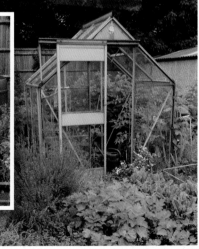

Plant directly into greenhouse borders

"a greenhouse allows you to grow heat-loving crops"

Cold frames

Some allotments do not allow greenhouses, limiting you to using cold frames or plastic mini-greenhouses, which, nonetheless, have many benefits. Cold frames are low to the ground and perfect for acclimatizing seedlings to outdoor temperatures after they have germinated. They can also be used to protect early sown crops in spring from frosts, prolonging the growing season. Mini greenhouses tend to be tall and narrow, and just large enough to grow two or three cordon tomatoes, peppers, chillies or aubergines.

Temporary covers Lightweight growing tents can be placed over crops outside, giving the benefits of a greenhouse on a small scale.

Mini greenhouse Where space is limited, collapsible plastic greenhouses are ideal for growing heat-loving crops, such as tomatoes.

Plastic covers The advantage of clear plastic is that, unlike glass, it doesn't shatter making it safer when children are around.

Wooden frames

Cold frames can be bought as kits, but they are just as easy to make yourself. The base can be made from bricks or wood, and an old window frame can be used as the lid. These can be permanent or temporary features.

Kits Cold frame kits come in a wide range of sizes to suit your needs, and are usually quick and easy to put together.

Recycled Reclaimed window frames are ideal for making cold frames, as are glass cupboard doors, and large picture frames.

Homemade (see p.50) This cold frame has been made from the sides of an old shed, and the lid was salvaged from a skip.

Project
Cold frame

A cold frame is an unheated box with a hinged glass lid that offers plants protection from rain, wind, and cold. They are most useful in spring for hardening off plants, but are also used for sowing seeds and winter protection. This one is made almost entirely of salvaged materials.

MATERIALS & TOOLS

- old window frame, shiplap wood, 4 corner posts, handles, battens, screws, nails, hinges, weed mat
- hammer, drill, screwdriver, staple gun, clamps, saw

Ensure that the angled cuts match, otherwise the lid may not close properly. It is easier to mark the boards before removing them to cut.

step 3

Strengthen the top of the frame by screwing on four strips of batten.

step 2

The rear panel should be slightly higher than the front to make the most of the sun, and to ensure rainwater doesn't settle on the lid.

G-clamps are useful for holding the frame together squarely while the boards are screwed into place.

Slot the timber tightly together and screw into place. Brush any dirt off the slats.

step 1

1   The dimensions of the cold frame are dictated by the size of the lid so measure it first. Saw the timber to length and cut the corner posts to the right height.

2   Assemble a pair of opposite sides first. This will make screwing together the final two sides far easier.

3   Having assembled the entire base of the frame, the top board on either side now needs to be cut at an angle so that the front is lower than the back.

Ventilation catch

It's vital that the cold frame can be easily ventilated, otherwise it will fill with stale air and overheat, causing plants to wither on hot days. The gap to allow for fresh air need not be more than about 5cm (2in).

Ventilation catch

An old hinge and an offcut of wood can be used to create a basic but effective ventilation catch.

The window frame can be slightly larger than the base to offer more protection at the edges from driving rain.

4 To prevent weeds growing up through the frame, staple a sheet of weed matting to the base.

5 Attach the window to the frame with sturdy hinges. If the timber is not very thick, fit the hinges at the corners, screwing into the posts for maximum strength.

The hinged lid of a cold frame makes tending the plants very easy. The size and location of the frame needs to be carefully considered to ensure all areas can be easily reached.

Lid support

There are various ways of holding open the lid of the frame while tending the plants. A length of batten and a simple catch made from a block of wood have been used here, although a salvaged window catch would work just as well.

Window catch

Cloches

Cloches are traditionally used in the vegetable garden to protect seedlings that need a little extra warmth early in the season. They are also useful for warming the soil in spring before planting or sowing, which results in faster growth compared to plants on uncovered soil.

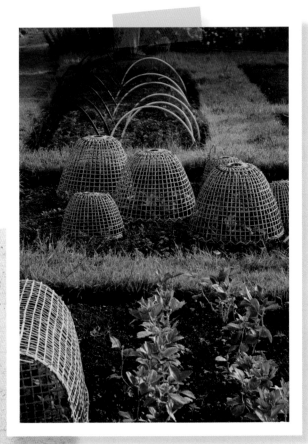

Types of cloche

The word cloche means "bell" in French and although traditional cloches are bell-shaped, there are many shapes and sizes available. Most people use "tunnel cloches", which consist of strong, clear polythene, stretched over wire hoops. These can be made large enough to cover whole rows of crops.

◆ **VENTILATION** is important when using a cloche to prevent the plants overheating when the sun comes out. Crops will also need extra watering, as the rain cannot reach the roots while the plants are growing under cover.

Bamboo cloches These open cloches are ideal for protecting plants from larger pests, such as birds and rabbits, and from wind damage.

Traditional glass cloches

Plastic tunnel cloche

Modern plastic dome cloche

Homemade cloches

Although cloches are widely sold and there are many designs to pick from, it can be just as easy to make your own, and is certainly more cost effective. Tunnel cloches are simple to make using lengths of old hosepipe to form the supporting loops, while small panes of glass can be propped together to provide an effective shelter for plants. Clear plastic bottles are ideal to cover small plants –just cut off the bases.

Homemade cloche made from old panes of glass and sticks

Bottle bases protect against pests

Storage system Keep your homemade bottle cloches tidy by threading them onto bamboo canes stuck into the ground. This stops them blowing around in the wind.

Project Hanging basket cloche

step **1**

step **2**

step **3**

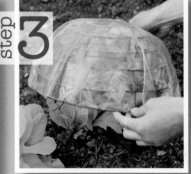

1 A simple cloche can be made from the frame of an old hanging basket. Wrap it in polythene or fleece and wire it to the frame.

2 Hold the polythene stretched reasonably tightly and cut off the surplus material so that the cloche is neat and tidy.

3 Place the cloche over seedlings for protection when frosty weather is predicted. Peg it down to hold it in place.

feeding & mulching

fertilizers & mulch • granular food • tomato food • making liquid comfrey • composting & compost bins • a recycled compost bin

Fertilizers & mulch

step 5

Keeping your plants well fed and mulched will encourage healthy plants, which in turn will provide you with abundant crops through the year. Adding fertilizers to the soil provides vital nutrients that may be lacking, particularly if other crops have been grown there previously. Mulching helps to improve the quality of the soil, suppresses weeds and retains moisture.

Fertilizer Always wear gloves when scattering fertilizer on the soil and read the manufacturer's instructions. You may also need to wear a dust mask.

Mulching

A variety of materials can be used for mulching, including well-rotted manure and garden compost.

Mulch seedlings Use well-rotted manure or garden compost to mulch around young seedlings. This retains moisture and suppresses weeds.

◆ **FRUIT TREES** and bushes are usually mulched in early spring. Take care that the mulch does not come into direct contact with the trunk, as this will eventually rot the tree, causing it to die. When applying mulch, spread it out in a circle to the edge of the leaf canopy and to a depth of 5cm (2in).

◆ **VEGETABLE BEDS** can be mulched in the autumn when they are empty. This gives time for the mulch to rot into the soil before you plant in spring.

◆ **APPLY MULCH** around seedlings and other plants to retain moisture and prevent weeds from germinating.

Granular feeds

Add fertilizer to the planting hole of fruit bushes to ensure the plant has the necessary nutrients when it starts growing. Controlled-release fertilizer releases its nutrients as the soil warms up, whereas slow-release fertilizer is gradually released into the soil.

Sprinkle granular fertilizer into the hole

Position the plant in the hole

The feed will slowly dissolve into the soil

How to apply fertilizers

Fertilizers usually come in liquid, granular or powder form. Liquid forms should be diluted in a watering can, whereas granules and powder are usually sprinkled from a measuring spoon at the recommended rate. Add fertilizer to the soil before you apply any mulch. Sprinkle it over the surface then rake it in lightly before you sow seed. Always wear gloves when you are handling powdered and granular feeds and always read the manufacturer's instructions carefully before use. Avoid feeding plants in direct sunlight as the combination of sun and fertilizer can scorch them.

Liquid Some powdered feeds need to be diluted in a watering can. Stir well with an old stick before applying the feed.

Use a tube Some feeds can be poured down a tube or plastic bottle to ensure the liquid reaches the roots where the nutrients are needed most.

Raking in Before you do any planting, lightly rake a general-purpose granular fertilizer into the soil.

No rose Most fertilizers work best when applied to the roots. Use a watering can without a rose for precision.

"**Tomato** feed is high in potassium and can be used to **feed fruiting** and vegetable plants"

Tomato feed

This must be diluted with water in a watering can. It is high in potassium and can be used to feed all fruiting vegetable plants – not just tomatoes – in order to improve colour and flavour. Start feeding weekly after the first flowers have appeared in summer.

Carefully measure out the feed

Add it to a clean watering can

Dilute to the recommended rate

Project
Liquid comfrey

Comfrey is regarded as something of a wonder plant, as it can easily be made into a liquid feed, packed full of essential nutrients to give to your veg. Plant a small clump and it will rapidly spread, providing you with an abundance of free, natural fertilizer for your plants.

MATERIALS & TOOLS

- comfrey plant, water
- two clean plastic milk bottles with lids, secateurs, watering can, sieve

Ensure that the cuttings you take are no longer than the container you plan to use to store the liquid fertilizer.

step 1

step 2

Clean, plastic 2-litre (3½-pint) milk bottles are ideal for this purpose. Insert five or six cuttings per bottle.

Easy to grow

Although comfrey can be grown from seed, it is far easier to grow it from cuttings. Fortunately, on an allotment you will easily and quickly find a source. Best of all are root cuttings, ideally planted while dormant. However, even the weakest-looking cutting will grow with suitable care.

Comfrey is so easy to grow that it can be difficult to eradicate, should you choose to at a later stage. It is a very vigorous plant and, on smaller plots, it is best grown in large containers to prevent it spreading.

1   Leaves from an established comfrey plant can be harvested four or five times a year, late spring to autumn. Cut stems that are about 20cm (8in) long to fit into a 2-litre (3½-pint) milk bottle. Stems can be harvested from anywhere on the plant as regrowth is usually fast.

2   Stuff the cuttings into the milk bottles, which should be clean, have tight-fitting lids, and necks large enough to squeeze the cuttings through. Bottles that have handles will make pouring easier later.

step **3**

How to use

Comfrey fertilizer (often called comfrey tea) can be used much like any other liquid feed. Tomatoes and courgettes in particular benefit from its use, and the cut stems are traditionally used to line a trench before planting potatoes. It can also be used as an "activator" in your compost bin to speed up the breakdown of the contents.

step **4**

Store for four to five weeks; the leaves will rot down and the mixture will be very pungent.

3 Fill the bottle with tap water to within a inch of the top.

4 Close the lid tightly and give the bottle a good shake, to make sure all the leaves have been agitated.

5 After a month or so, strain the liquid through a sieve to remove the foliage and pour the liquid into clean, plastic containers to store for use on the allotment.

step **5**

You may find it easier to strain the comfrey feed into a watering can and then to pour it into clean containers.

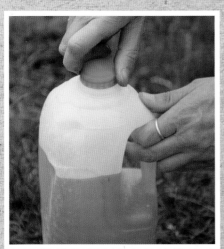

Before using, dilute the comfrey feed to about 1 part fertilizer, 10 parts water. The darker the feed, the more you should dilute it.

Composting & compost bins

step 5

Well-rotted compost is an essential ingredient on the allotment. Whether dug in or used as mulch, it lightens clay soils, improves moisture retention on sandy soils, and supplies valuable nutrients to your crops. It takes time to get a composting system going and it may be months before your first batch is ready, so start as soon as you can.

Useful screening Compost bins can look unsightly, but are easily screened with trellis, flowers, or by climbing crops, such as beans.

Why compost?

There are many good reasons to make your own compost, the most obvious being that it provides an excellent soil improver, better than any you can buy, and almost completely free. Composting also provides the means to easily dispose of kitchen waste, lawn and hedge clippings, and plant debris from the allotment that you would otherwise have to throw away. Making your own compost means you know what is going into the soil, and ultimately into your crops, which is important if you grow organically. Compost heaps also provide habitat and will attract beneficial insects, such as beetles and centipedes.

Correct proportions
When making compost, aim to mix two parts carbon-rich materials, such as dried leaves and wood chippings, with one part nitrogen-rich leafy material, such as grass clippings and plant waste.

Turning the heap

Compost heaps should be turned about once a month to incorporate air into the material, which speeds up the process of decomposition. Turning involves digging out the material at the bottom of the heap and placing it on top. The compost is ready to use when it is dark brown, with a crumbly soil-like texture, and has a smell like damp woodland. It should not smell unpleasant or feel slimy.

Turning the compost

DO'S & DON'TS

- Do have more than one compost bin on the go.
- Make sure compost is covered to prevent material washing away.
- Turn the compost once a month.
- Add water to the heap if it appears dry during summer.
- Don't add diseased plant material.
- Don't add meat or cooked food.

Types of bins

There is a wide range of compost bins available to buy, usually made of plastic or wood. They either come as kits or ready-made. Choose a size and design that suits your needs; have two bins if possible, so you can be emptying one, while filling the other. Some allotment societies and local authorities provide compost bins free or at a discounted price, so make enquiries before buying your own. Compost bins are also easy make. All you need is a large, sturdy container that will hold the material, but also keeps out excess rainfall, allows air to circulate, and drains at the base.

Recycled This compost bin was built from old wooden pallets, and can be made in about an hour. (See Project, pp.62–63)

Sectional Some compost bins consist of interlocking sections that can be stacked up gradually as more material is added to the heap.

Drum types These large, plastic bins are a popular choice. They are easy to set up, and come with a lid and an access hatch at the base.

Tumble bins This type of bin is designed to rotate. The tumbling action mixes the contents with air and accelerates the composting process.

Slotted bins The holes in this plastic compost bin allow the air to circulate, which speeds up the process of decomposition.

Recycled tyres If you can obtain free tyres, it is cheap and very simple to make this bin by stacking them in a pile.

Mini tumbler This small, rotating bin is ideal for making compost quickly where space is limited. Turn the drum once a week.

Builders' bags Green waste will rot down in most containers. These strong, woven, plastic bags are useful for creating good compost.

Project
Compost bin

Making your own compost is the best way of recycling garden and kitchen waste, and no allotment is complete without at least one compost bin. Well-rotted compost makes an excellent soil improver, and will keep your plot fertile and productive. The compost bin made here uses recycled materials and is very easy to construct.

Fix wooden battens at the corners of the bin to prevent the sides pushing apart. Use a G-clamp to hold them in place, then screw them in firmly.

step **3**

MATERIALS & TOOLS

- four pallets, ideally the same size, two gate hinges, offcuts of batten or planks, selection of screws
- screwdriver, hammer, G-clamps, hand saw

step **2**

Use an assistant to hold the pallets in place, although if the ground is reasonably level, they should stand up on their own.

Most pallets have chunky blocks at each corner. These are ideal for driving screws into, offering more support than the thin planks.

step **1**

1   Find a suitable and accessible location for the bin, then roughly level the ground to make sure that the pallets will stand level, and position the four pallets in place.

2   Once you are satisfied that the pallets are sitting squarely, drive two or three heavy-gauge screws in at each corner, top and bottom, making sure that the pallets line up neatly at the edges.

3   Strengthen the joints using offcuts of timber, screwing them in place. When it is full, there may be considerable weight inside the compost bin, so it should be properly supported.

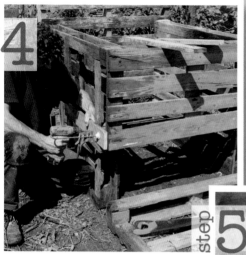

step 4

Carpet cover

To prevent the contents of the compost bin from getting too wet, cover the top using a tarpaulin or, for this project, some old carpet. Simply drape it over the top and secure it in place with some string so it does not get blown away. In warm spells, remove the cover and check the compost hasn't become dry, and add water if necessary.

step 5

step 6

Ensure that the access hatch opens and closes easily. To hold it shut, drive a stake into the ground in front of it (see above) or place bricks or large stones there.

4 This particular bin has a hinged door at the bottom of one side to give easy access to the compost when it is ready.

5 Cut off the lower portion of one pallet to serve as the hatch, and use a sturdy pair of gate hinges to reattach it.

6 Finally, attach a rudimentary catch to hold the hatch open when the compost is removed. A piece of batten held in place with a single, loosely-tightened screw is ideal.

The door, once fully opened, can be held in place with the wooden catch, which simply swivels into place.

Although pallets are very sturdy, they will gradually decay, especially when used to make a compost heap. Check the joints every year, and if the structure seems to have weakened, build a replacement. Avoid using wood preservatives, which may taint the compost.

step 6

watering & weeding

watering methods •
water supply • weeds
& weeding • disposing
of weeds

Watering methods

Fruit and vegetable plants depend on regular watering in order to grow. Lack of water is the most common reason for plants dying. During dry periods in the summer it may be necessary to visit the allotment daily to check on young seedlings and water them. Install water-saving devices such as water butts to maximize water conservation.

Water butts Collect rainwater by attaching guttering to the shed or greenhouse roof, and attach downpipes that feed into barrels or water butts.

Water tank and cistern Many allotment sites have a water tank with a cistern. Every time water is scooped out, it automatically refills itself.

Getting it right

Giving your plants the right amount of water is critical. They will die if they don't receive enough, yet they can also suffer if they are overwatered. If fruit is overwatered it can split, particularly when close to harvest time. Vegetables often rot in damp conditions, and seedlings can suffer from fungal diseases. The simplest way to see if your plant needs watering is to stick your finger in the soil; if it feels dry, then it needs water. Give plants a thorough soak every few days to ensure that water gets right down to the deep roots.

Standpipes Some sites provide a standpipe to which hosepipes and irrigation systems can be connected, making watering easier.

Better watering

On hot days, water in the morning or the evening when it is cooler. This gives the moisture an opportunity to soak slowly into the soil. Watering at midday in full sun can cause the leaves to scorch, and water quickly evaporates, rather than soaking in. Check the individual requirements of your crops as some don't like alkaline water. This is particularly the case with blueberries and cranberries, which should only be watered with rainwater. Soil type, especially how well it drains, also affects how often plants will need to be watered.

Watering with a rose Traditional cans are useful for controlling the amount of water given to individual plants. Attaching a rose to the end of the spout gives a gentle flow, ideal when watering young plants.

Puddle watering Creating a hollow or sump around plants acts as a reservoir, allowing water to pool around their bases and slowly soak down to the roots. However, make sure that the roots are still covered by soil, otherwise they will dry out even quicker, and can be eaten by pests.

Using a hosepipe This is the quickest method of watering large areas, but it can be wasteful. Direct the hose at the base of each plant so the water reaches the roots and doesn't splash wastefully off the leaves.

Using a homemade funnel Cut the bases off plastic bottles and bury the mouth-ends in the soil, next to plants. This creates a funnel that will channel the water directly to the roots.

Additional help

There are various irrigation methods and devices available to make watering easier. They help if you can't water the plot every day.

Bottle reservoirs Make holes in the caps of water-filled bottles and leave them to drip into the soil.

Pouch reservoirs This method involves a large water-filled pouch suspended over crops that slowly waters them via a thin tube.

WATER WISELY

- Consider others when using communal taps.
- Check whether the soil is dry to avoid water wastage.
- Water in the morning or evening.
- Install water butts to minimize using mains water.
- Don't waste water – only water around the root system of your plants.

step 6 Weeds & weeding

Weeds are a bane of the allotment grower's life, competing with crops for water, nutrients, and light. Keep them under control, as they can smother smaller crops, and can be hard to eradicate once established.

PERENNIAL WEEDS

Perennial weeds regrow each year from their root system and are the hardest to get rid of. Most have a deep root system and include:

- dandelion
- bindweed
- ground elder
- perennial nettle
- ragwort
- dock

ANNUAL WEEDS

Annual weeds grow, set seed and die within a year. They usually have a shallow root system and are easy to hoe off or dig out. They include:

- hairy bittercress
- shepherd's purse
- groundsel
- annual meadow grass
- goosegrass

Preventing weeds

It is impossible to avoid weeds on the allotment, particularly if they aren't being controlled on neighbouring plots from where they can easily spread. To help prevent them, cover any bare areas of soil, such as paths, with weed-suppressant membrane. On new beds, consider covering the soil with black plastic and plant your crops through it. Regularly mulching crops deters weeds and also feeds your plants, so they are less affected by the competition. Cultivating the soil also helps to limit weeds. Although this brings weed seeds to the surface, where they will germinate, the seedlings will soon be unearthed and dug into the soil. Routine weeding also helps prevent future weeds by stopping them from setting seeds.

Draw hoe This is used for removing shallow-rooted weeds. Pull it through the surface of the soil towards yourself.

Hand fork This small tool can be used for digging out weeds without damaging the roots of adjacent vegetables.

Dutch hoe Push this hoe through the surface of the soil to sever the stems of shallow-rooting weeds.

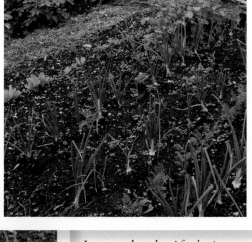

Leave weeds to dry After hoeing, annual weeds can be left in the sun for a few days to dry out before collecting them up.

Speedy removal Hoeing is a quick way to remove annual weeds. Use a long-handled hoe to reach into the beds easily.

Composting

Annual weeds can be put in the compost heap immediately, although avoid adding any that have set seed. Perennial weeds can be composted, but must be completely dead first.

Collect the weeds Avoid immediately adding freshly dug up perennial roots to the compost, as they will regenerate and spread in the heap.

Dry in the sun (see Project, p.162) Perennial weeds should be collected up and left on a rack to dry in the sun for a few weeks before adding to the compost heap.

> ## "weeds are a bane
> ### of the allotment grower's life,
> ## competing with crops"

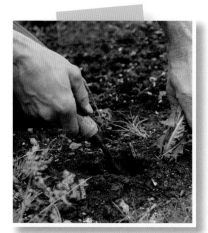

Dandelion grubber Dandelions have a deep taproot, which should be removed entirely to prevent it re-sprouting.

Garden fork Use a fork to dig out perennial weeds. A spade may slice up the roots, causing a bigger problem.

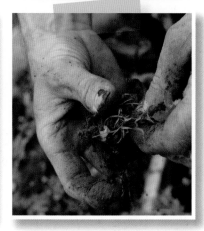

Hand weeding Weed between individual plants by pulling the weed seedlings out by hand. Pull them before they establish.

step 7

what to grow

crops to suit your soil
& aspect • soil quality
• choosing crops •
flowers for cutting

Step 7 Which crops will suit your soil & aspect

Some plants have specific requirements and will only grow successfully if they have the right conditions. Take time to check what they need and carefully read labels on seed packets and plants to ensure you are planting them in an environment where they will thrive.

Alkaline soil

Where the soil is acidic, some plants are unable to access certain nutrients in it, which will lead to poor plant growth. Lime can be added, which will make the soil more alkaline – and increase its pH. If you are unsure what the pH of your soil is, buy a simple test kit.

Luxuriant leaves To produce a healthy crop like this, carefully check the soil and light levels on your plot before planting.

Soil quality

Do not despair if the quality of your soil is not ideal; it can be improved by adding organic matter, such as well-rotted manure or garden compost. Poor-draining soil can be improved by adding horticultural grit and sand. If excess alkalinity is the problem, there is very little that can be done to make the soil suitable for acid-loving plants, such as blueberries. The best solution is to grow acid-lovers in raised beds or containers, where you can then provide them with the perfect soil. Raised beds can be made cheaply from recycled material and are easy to construct, while a bonus with containers is that they can be moved in and out of the sun as required.

The cabbage family, including broccoli and sprouts, prefers a slightly alkaline soil and will be less prone to clubroot (see p.235).

Acidic soil

Some plants will only grow in acidic soil. If your soil is very alkaline, the plants will need to be grown in containers or raised beds filled with ericaceous compost. If the soil has a neutral pH or lower, then it may be possible to acidify it with sulphur chips.

Blueberries are very fussy and will only grow in acidic soil with a pH lower than 5.5.

Cranberries have similar acidic requirements to blueberries, but prefer very damp soil.

Potatoes are less prone to the fungal disease potato scab when grown in slightly acid soil.

Full sun

Most plants prefer full sun. Mediterranean-type plants, such as tomatoes, peppers, aubergines, and squashes in particular, need lots of light and warmth. Don't forget that plants in the sun also require plenty of water.

Aubergines must be harvested while the skins are still shiny.

Tomatoes are easy to grow and will crop all through summer.

Peppers will grow happily in pots if space is at a premium.

Chillies add colour to the allotment and are easy to grow.

Strawberries will fruit from late spring until the first frosts.

Basil is an annual herb that you can easily grow from seed.

Apples are available in hundreds of varieties, some on dwarfing rootstock.

Pears taste most flavoursome if eaten within days of picking.

Peaches should be fan-trained against south-facing walls.

Figs fruit more freely if the roots of the tree are restricted.

Shade

A few plants will tolerate light shade or even full shade. Cooking apples, gooseberries and redcurrants will grow on north-facing walls, while rhubarb is ideal for a shady corner of the plot. Leafy crops and the cabbage family will cope with moderate shade.

> "**Leafy** crops cope well with **moderate** shade"

Gooseberries are sweetest when harvested in early summer.

Redcurrants can be planted against a wall if space is limited.

Cooking apples can be grown in shadier sites than dessert apples.

The cabbage family will provide a crop all year round.

Swiss chard can be harvested as a baby leaf crop or as mature leaves.

Choosing crops

The most exciting aspect of having your own allotment is choosing what delicious fruit and vegetables you are going to be growing for your family and friends. Seed companies and garden centres have a huge range of crops on offer to suit everybody's personal taste. Be adventurous and grow things you would never find in a supermarket.

TO GROW...	easy
TO BUY...	expensive
SPACE NEEDED...	small

Buying versus growing Some common crops are so cheap to buy that it isn't worth wasting space growing them on the plot.

You can save yourself a fortune by growing some of the crops that are expensive to buy, yet can be grown easily for the cost of a few packets of seeds or plants. Year after year and for very little outlay, you could be picking an abundance of those delicious crops that you consider a real luxury. For example, raspberries are very expensive to buy, yet you will be able to harvest punnet-loads if you grow your own. Similarly, courgettes produce huge crops from just one plant but are costly in the shops.

- beetroot
- broad beans
- Brussels sprouts
- calabrese
- celeriac
- courgettes
- French beans
- herbs
- leeks
- lettuce
- mangetout
- peas
- mixed salad leaves
- purple and white sprouting broccoli
- radishes
- runner beans
- spring onions
- shallots
- spinach
- spinach beet and chard
- turnips
- soft fruit
- rhubarb

beetroot

lettuce

raspberries   *mangetout*

spring onions

"cheap to grow, **expensive** to buy**"**

🌱	TO GROW...	easy
💷	TO BUY...	cheap
▪	SPACE NEEDED...	large

Some crops found in abundance in the shops are often extremely cheap, and therefore may not be worth the effort of growing yourself. Maincrop potatoes, for example, take up a lot of space and, although there are some great varieties available, you may decide that your space could be better used by planting more unusual or expensive-to-buy crops. Onions are another example of a crop that is inexpensive in the shops and takes up a lot of space. Consider your priorities carefully before deciding which crops to grow.

onions

garlic

cabbage

parsnips

sweet potato

- cabbages
- carrots
- celery
- garlic
- onions
- melons
- outdoor tomatoes
- parsnips
- peas
- potatoes
- pumpkins
- squash
- cauliflower
- swedes
- sweet potatoes

"cheap to buy so less worth growing"

🌱	TO GROW...	various
💷	TO BUY...	you can't
▪	SPACE NEEDED...	various

There are certain specialist crops that you just won't find in the shops. This is usually because they have a limited shelf life or because farmers don't consider it worthwhile growing them, but many are worth trying. Japanese wineberries, for example, produce tiny, delicious, blackberry-like berries that have the sweetest flavour ever. Courgette flowers don't last long enough to sell in the shops, but can be picked and fried in batter.

Romanesco broccoli

- beetroot leaves — earthy spinach substitute
- Chinese artichokes — hard to harvest commercially, but easily grown at home
- courgette flowers — too fragile to be transported
- hop shoots — used like asparagus
- Japanese wineberry — small fruits, costly to pick
- oriental flowering kales — flowers deteriorate quickly after picking
- pea tendrils — costly to harvest and pack
- radish seedpods — good for snacks and stir-fries
- Romanesco broccoli — easily bruised in transit
- sorrel — costly to pick
- tomatillo — doesn't get blight
- unripe wheat berries — used in some continental recipes

courgette flowers

"money can't buy these"

Flowers

Growing a range of flowers alongside your fruit and vegetable crops on the allotment has many advantages. Not only will the flowers attract many beneficial pollinators that will also visit your other crops, but you will also have a supply of cut flowers for the house. You can grow your flowers in dedicated flower beds or among your fruit and veg, where they will add colour, beauty and scent to your plot.

Sweet peas and lavender
Sweet peas growing up bamboo canes and lavender used as underplanting will waft their scent in the air.

Companion planting Flowers can be grown as companions to vegetable plants, making the vegetables healthier by deterring pests and diseases from attacking the crops. Companion flowers will also attract pollinating insects.

Shrubs and climbers

Shrubs and climbers can be used to add height and permanent structure to your plot. Roses are perfect, with rambler types scrambling up trellises and through flower beds, giving the plot a wild and rustic feel, while shrub roses and hybrid tea roses can be used as cut flowers or simply to beautify the area. Winter-flowering shrubs are especially welcome as they attract pollinating insects to the site.

◆ **HERBACEOUS PERENNIALS** are a good investment as, once planted, they will appear each year before dying back during the winter and reappearing in spring. They can be grown as cut flowers or to scent the area and make it look pretty.

◆ **ANNUALS** are perfect for creating a quick splash of colour for the cost of just a few packets of seeds. There is a very wide range of plants to choose from, including favourites such as sweet peas and sunflowers, both of which are great for cutting.

Flowers for cutting

If you are growing flowers to cut for the house, it is easier to grow them in a "cut flower" bed rather than mixing them with other plants. Most flowers require fertile, rich soil if they are to bloom prolifically, so add plenty of organic matter. Choose a range of varieties and you can have cut flowers for most of the year.

◆ **SPRING FLOWERS** could include daffodils and tulips; good summer choices are cosmos, roses, gladioli, sunflowers and sweetpeas; flowers for autumn are asters, chrysanthemums and dahlias; and for winter, holly for berries and witch hazel for stems.

Personalize your plot with flowers

Flowers are a wonderful expression of your personality and with such a range of shrubs and herbaceous perennials, it's easy to find something that you love. Plant them around seating areas to enjoy them in your down time.

Flowers for cutting If you are growing flowers for cutting it is easier to reach them if they are grown in rows. Remember to label them with their name and the date they were sown.

POLLINATION

Most flowers attract pollinating insects but some do the job better than others.

- **AVOID** double flowers as bees cannot get inside the flowers easily.
- **SELECT** a range of flowers that will provide blooms for most of the year.
- **CHOOSE** native flowers and avoid bedding plants.
- **PICK** flowers that are blue, purple, violet, white and yellow, as bees have good colour vision and are particularly attracted to these.

Hide your compost bin

As well as adding scent and colour to your plot, flowering shrubs and herbaceous perennials can be used to screen unsightly areas such as compost bins, cold frames and polytunnels. Ideally, choose evergreen plants like sarcococca and holly, as these will create an all-year-round screen. Alternatively, erect fences or trellis made from recycled materials and grow climbers such as honeysuckle, roses and clematis up them. For summer screening from eyesores, grow tall flowers, such as rows of delphiniums, verbascums, sunflowers or sweetpeas.

step 8

creating a style

your style • seating & socializing • making a bench • herbs & the kitchen garden • children • a herb parterre • chickens & bees

step

8 Your style

One of the exciting aspects of having an allotment is the chance to stamp your individuality on it. Your style can be as unusual and different as you like, the only restriction being your imagination. Revel in the freedom of creating something that's you, then sit back and enjoy the results.

Polytunnels Used to grow crops that need extra protection, a polytunnel also adds a laid-back feel to the allotment.

Define your style

Choose a style that will suit your personality. Don't follow design advice in books word for word, but instead look within yourself for inspiration. Are you a formal or informal sort of person? Do your tastes veer towards the modern or the traditional? Some people like to have everything perfectly manicured, with vegetables standing in immaculate straight lines and pristine bamboo canes geometrically spaced one from the next. Others like a riot of colour and shape, with beds overflowing with an abundance of vegetables, flowers and fruit. Yet others like to reflect their nationality or culture, perhaps growing crops that are traditionally eaten in their country of origin, or personalizing their plot with anything from a garden gnome to a seated Bhudda statue.

Geometry and texture The strong geometrical shape of this parterre creates a modern and contemporary feel, while the textural foliage of the herbs and edible crops adds a sensory dimension to the design.

Formal or informal? These cabbages in perfect straight lines add a touch of formality to the plot, but the purple and green also add a creative contrast of colours.

Mixing styles The style of this kitchen garden is informal with lots of plants packed closely together, yet the stark, sharp lines of the patio create an interesting contrast.

Community

If you're not sure you have time to manage an allotment, or don't feel confident about your horticultural skills, then you could consider getting involved with a local community garden. These are shared spaces where you garden on a communal piece of land in your neighbourhood with other like-minded individuals. It's a fantastic way to meet new friends, pick up tips and, of course, take home your own fruit and veg, without the responsibility of maintaining a whole plot.

Style compromise Working on a community allotment means tailoring your style ideas to suit everyone else involved.

Seating & socializing

Growing your own is not all about hard graft, digging and weeding; socializing and having fun with family, friends and fellow-gardeners helps to maintain a balance between work and play, and is one of the major perks of having a plot. Create comfortable seating areas for you to take well-earned breaks and entertain others.

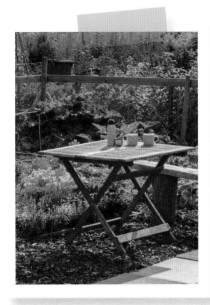

Making new friends

Most allotment sites will organize events to ensure you get to know your like-minded neighbours. Meeting others is a great way to exchange seeds and plants, but is also a valuable opportunity to get tips from some of the more experienced growers. Make sure you always have an extra cup of coffee in the flask for impromptu chats as people pass by your plot.

Time out Take time to relax and make new friends. Invite them over for a barbecue or even ask them to give you a hand with a job in return for you helping them out with one of theirs.

 PROJECT Bench

Make sure that the tops of the logs are level with each other so that the plank seat will sit flat without rocking.

Use lengths of timber to hold the logs in position temporarily, keeping the logs level and upright; remove once the concrete has cured.

1   It is important to do a trial run to see where your garden seat fits best. You should also ensure the logs are long enough to allow about 30cm (12in) to be bedded in concrete below ground.

2   Allow an additional 5–7.5cm (2–3in) around the circumference of the logs for the concrete bed and a similar depth beneath.

3   Firmly pack the concrete around the circumference of the logs, trying to minimize air pockets, then smooth the top with a trowel 5cm (2in) below ground level to leave some space for bark chips or similar material to cover the concrete when dry.

Storage and seating This recycled toolbox combines a handy storage space with a useful seating area that allows you to take a break from working on the plot.

Placing your seats

Think carefully about where you want to place your seating areas. If your dream is to have a quiet, secluded place where you can spend your weekend afternoons resting in the midday sun, you will need to make a space somewhere in a quiet corner out of sight of the prying eyes of passers-by. However, if you like perching on a bench, watching the world go by and chatting to neighbours as they go about their business, then a prominent seat near the path will be a better choice for you.

Sunny spot Before creating a seating area, check to see whether it is in the sun or shade. Consider building screens and overhead pergolas if you are not a sun-lover.

Time to relax Consider old-fashioned deck chairs for your seating. They are comfortable to lie back in and you can easily fold them up and store them in the shed.

Positioning Lay your seat across the logs and mark it with the locations of the two heavy-duty screws that must be drilled into each log. Drill a pilot hole for each one and tighten the screws fully with a wrench so that the heads are just a fraction below the surface of the seat.

Cosy corner Everybody needs the occasional slice of peace and solitude, away from the madding crowd. On this allotment, the owner has erected recycled fence panels to create a private seating area.

Herbs & the kitchen garden

Growing herbs adds another dimension to the veg garden. When used in formal parterres they can create rich tapestries of colours and patterns. They can also be grown for their beautiful flowers, for culinary use, or simply for their aromatic qualities.

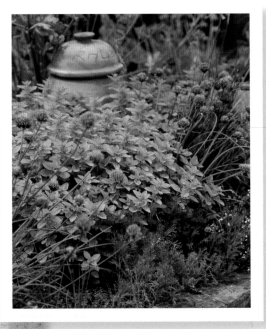

Where to grow herbs

Herbs can either be grown separately in a herb garden or interplanted among vegetables and flowers. Fennel, with its stately umbels, blends in beautifully in a flower bed. Low-growing plants such as chamomile and thyme make attractive underplanting around the base of fruit trees, or they can be used to create herb lawns and paths. Many herbs have useful medicinal properties, but make sure you seek professional advice before using them to cure ailments. In terms of design, the huge range of textures, colours and habit exhibited by herbs provides an exciting palette for gardeners to use.

Edging Herbs such as rosemary, lavender or, in this case, chives, can be used to edge beds or weave intricate patterns to form strong structures and geometrical shapes.

"In formal parterres herbs create rich tapestries of colours and patterns"

A lettuce parterre The interplanting of herbs and lettuces creates a garden that is pleasing to the eye as well as good to eat. Keep sowing lettuce in pots so you can replace those you have harvested.

Edging with box (see Project p.87) Box is the most commonly used plant for edging parterres and herb gardens as it is compact and evergreen. Prune when the risk of frosts is over.

Children

Gardening is a wonderful hobby to involve your children in. Not only does it provide some great physical exercise, but it also teaches them about where food comes from and encourages them to eat a more healthy and varied diet.

Containers Start children off with small growing spaces, such as compost-filled containers; that way they will not get overwhelmed by a large space.

Community gardens Children love the social aspect of learning how to garden. There's nothing more fun than getting messy on the plot with friends.

How to inspire children

Children like to see quick results so choose fast-growing crops such as "cut-and-come-again" salad leaves, radishes and baby carrots. Also, get them involved with choosing food they will enjoy eating, such as strawberries, raspberries, carrots and potatoes.

◆ **MOST CHILDREN LOVE** the messy aspects of working on the soil, so consider setting up a wormery or getting them to turn the compost. They also enjoy picking all the slimy slugs, snails and even caterpillars off the plants. Many allotment sites have after-school clubs, which is a fantastic way to get children excited and inspired about growing their own food. It's also a great opportunity to pass on your newly acquired culinary and horticultural expertise to the next generation.

Safety first

Make sure the allotment is a safe environment for children to garden in. Check the site over and remove any broken glass or trip hazards. Cover bamboo canes with protectors to prevent eye injuries. There are some creative methods of doing this (see right).

Plastic connector

Flexible tubing

Small bottles

Snail shells

Project
Herb parterre

A traditional parterre is an ornamental herb, flower or vegetable bed edged with low, tightly clipped evergreen hedging. This is a novel way to introduce some variety and additional colour to your allotment, while remaining practical and providing a good opportunity to grow some useful culinary herbs.

step 3

This parterre follows a very simple yet practical design, providing four triangular beds for the herbs.

step 2

step 1

1   Prepare the plot thoroughly by digging in plenty of organic matter, then cover the plot with a generous layer of well-rotted compost and rake it over so it looks fine and crumbly.

2   Having decided on the plan of your parterre, peg out the plot using bamboo canes and run string lines across to section it off.

3   Do a trial run before planting, placing plants on the ground and moving them around until you are happy with the final layout.

Planting mint

Mint is often found in herb gardens and its leaves add flavour to very many recipes. However, take great care where you plant it as it is very invasive and can take over the whole garden. To contain its fast-growing and vigorous roots, plant mint in a submerged pot, leaving the top of the pot slightly above ground level.

step 4

MATERIALS & TOOLS
- string line, bamboo canes, bucket, selection of plants
- hand trowel, tape measure

Careful planning should ensure that once the herbs reach maturity, a fairly uniform ground covering will be achieved.

step 5

4 Box is a popular choice for the edging. Make a neat hole for each plant and firm some extra soil around them as you go. Maintain an even spacing between the plants as this will help to achieve the formal appearance of your parterre.

5 Once the box or other edging plants are in place, the herbs can be planted. Allocate a specific herb to each section of the parterre or follow a theme.

Once the box hedging has settled and started to bulk out, it can be trimmed to shape as desired. Wait until the risk of frosts is over in early summer before using a hedge-trimmer or edging shears to trim back the new growth.

Chickens

Keeping chickens is a wonderfully rewarding hobby and will supply you with delicious fresh eggs most days. Before committing to chickens, however, you need to make sure that you can visit the plot at least twice a day to feed and water them, and to shut them up at night.

Keeping chickens

When you are working down on the plot, let the chickens out of their run and allow them to peck over vegetable beds that have been harvested. They are fantastic at weeding, devouring small pests and lightly scratching up the soil. One of the other benefits of keeping chickens is that they will give you a regular supply of chicken manure, which makes a wonderful soil improver. Make sure it is well rotted down before adding it to the soil as its rich qualities will burn plant roots. Some allotment committees don't allow chickens to be kept on site, so do check before purchasing them.

Sheltered home Chickens need a sheltered building with a perch to sit on. Their run should be as large as possible and fox-proof.

Chicken breeds There are many breeds to choose from. Seek advice for the one that meets your needs and also suits your conditions.

Chicken houses

Chicken houses and arks come in all sorts of shapes and sizes and there are no hard-and-fast rules as to the perfect home. However, they need to be watertight and fox-proof and they must have a perch inside, as chickens like to sit high up on a bar rather than sitting on the floor. A chicken house also needs a separate nest area where the hens can lay their eggs. If your hens feel safe and happy, they will lay more eggs.

Bees

Keeping a hive or two of bees is not to everyone's taste. However, if you become a beekeeper, not only will you have a constant supply of your own honey, but the bees will pollinate your flowers, ensuring that you get bigger fruit and vegetable crops.

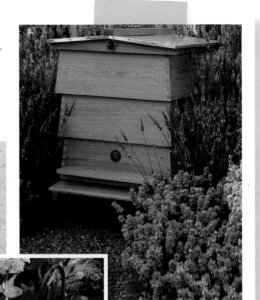

Buying bees

When you are considering buying bees, chat to your neighbours to ensure they are happy to have hives nearby. A promise of a jar or two of honey is usually enough to convince them. Position the entrance to the beehive away from paths or neighbouring plots so that nobody accidentally gets stung because they are in the flight path. Before buying your bees, go on a short training course to learn the basics. Local beekeeping societies regularly run evening courses to get you up and running.

"Encourage bees to your plot"

Flowers Surround your hive with a range of flowering plants that will encourage bees and other pollinating insects to visit.

Homemade Bees such as bumble and solitary bees will pollinate your plants. Encourage them to your plot by providing them with homemade homes.

Honey

Honey is made from the nectar collected by bees from the surrounding area. Although they will travel quite far in search of suitable plants, they would much rather forage closer to home, so choose a range of plants that will flower for as much of the year as possible. Bees will even forage during winter if the weather is mild enough. The honey will be a distillation of your fruit and vegetable beds in a jar. Perfect!

crop rotation

soil **fertility** • three- & four-year rotation • catch crops • intercropping • catch crop partners • intercropping partners

Crop rotation

When considering planting or sowing your first vegetables, it is a good idea to have a long-term plan. A basic understanding of where to plant your crops over the next three or four years is important for maximizing the space available and caring for the fertility of your soil.

The concept of crop rotation

This essential gardening technique can seem daunting and rather confusing at first, but it is actually a very simple concept. The idea is that annual crops are grown in a different section of the vegetable patch each year. By doing this, it avoids the problem of pests and diseases building up in the soil, which can happen if crops are grown in the same location two years running or more. For the purposes of crop rotation, the hundreds of vegetable crops have been categorized into three, or sometimes four, basic groups, as follows: root and potato crops, the cabbage family (or brassicas) and the pea and bean family (or legumes). So, in order to rotate the crops, in the second year the crops in Bed 1 go to Bed 3; those in Bed 3 go to Bed 2; and Bed 2 crops go to Bed 1 (see right).

Three-year rotation

Most people operate a three-year rotation programme, as this is the simplest one to manage. On a really small plot you can operate just two groups, which could be potatoes grouped with root crops, rotated with everything else. Some crops, such as pumpkins, lettuces and courgettes, suffer from fewer diseases and can be planted wherever there is space.

- Year 1: potatoes, tomatoes and root crops
- Year 2: peas and beans
- Year 3: cabbage family

Four-year rotation

For more advanced planning, a four-year crop rotation can be used, separating potatoes and tomatoes from root vegetables. Sadly, blight, which affects them both, is airborne and crop rotation won't prevent it.

- Year 1: potatoes and tomatoes
- Year 2: root vegetables
- Year 3: peas and beans
- Year 4: cabbage family

Benefits of rotation

One of the benefits of crop rotation is that it maximizes the amount of fertility available in the soil for specific groups of vegetables. For example, peas and beans fix nitrogen in the soil, so it makes sense to plant cabbages after peas and beans, as the cabbages' leafy growth thrives in nitrogen-rich soil. Similarly, peas like a deep soil, so plant those after your root crops have loosened the ground and broken up the soil somewhat.

Avoiding fresh manure Carrots don't appreciate growing in a freshly manured plot, so it is best to plant them after the cabbage group.

Pests and diseases Moving the crops each year prevents a build-up of diseases in the soil, but won't prevent slugs, snails and flying pests.

Control of weeds Use potatoes for the first year of crop rotation, as they help to break up the soil and should help to smother some weeds.

Bed 1 Potatoes and root vegetables are usually planted first, as this breaks up the soil and creates a nice deep root run for the crops that will follow them.

Bed 2 Peas and beans are legumes and store nitrogen in their root nodules. They are planted after the root vegetables and thrive in the deep soil vacated by root crops.

Bed 3 The cabbage family includes sprouts, broccoli, cauliflowers, cabbages and kale. These crops will thrive in the nitrogen-rich soil left by the legumes.

Don't rotate

Crop rotation is essentially for annual plants as perennials stay where they have been planted for a few years. This means that you do not have to include plants such as rhubarb, asparagus, perennial herbs and fruit trees or bushes in your crop-rotation plans. However, their long-term location should be factored in when planning which crops are going where.

Asparagus These delicious spears are usually grown in their own section of the allotment. Make sure the site is thoroughly prepared prior to planting, as they will be in the ground for a few years.

Rhubarb These colourful, leafy plants can get extremely large and will need quite a lot of space to grow to their full potential. Use them to fill those tricky shady corners, where they will thrive.

Fruit trees and bushes When planning the allotment it is a good idea to get the fruiting plants in first; they will form the structure of your allotment and other plants can be worked around them.

step 9

Catch crops & intercropping

Once you have worked out where your main crops are to go, you can turn your attention to growing catch crops and intercropping. These are good ways to maximize your space and benefit from some quick-result crops as a bonus.

Catch crops

This is a popular technique that involves sowing quick-growing crops in the bare soil between your larger, slower-growing crops before the slower crops reach full maturity. For example, you could sow some fast-growing salad leaves between your widely spaced, slower-growing cauliflowers. However, it is important to remember to harvest the fast-growing crops before they start to compete with the hungry larger plants for the nutrients in the soil.

Catch crop partners

Small, fast-growing crops include radishes, beetroot tops, rocket, salad leaves and spinach. Large, slower-growing crops are usually from the cabbage family. When planting main-crop plants, leave some extra space to allow room for catch crops in between.

PARTNERS

- sprouts with radishes
- cauliflower with lettuce
- cabbage with baby carrots
- kale with baby beetroot
- broccoli with baby turnip tops

Project Sweetcorn

Sweetcorn provides shade for the lettuce so the two crops are perfect parners.

Sprinkle lettuce seeds over the surface and water them using a can with a rose.

step 1

step 2

step 3

1 Being a wind-pollinated plant, sweetcorn should be grown in a grid rather than in rows. Use a stick to mark out the grid pattern.

2 Dig planting holes 45cm (18in) apart with a trowel, following your marked-out grid pattern, then plant the sweetcorn seedlings.

3 Scatter lettuce seed in between the sweetcorn. After germination, thin out the seedlings to give space for the lettuces to grow.

"Sow quick-growing crops after a main crop has been harvested"

Catch cropping

Intercropping

This is similar to growing catch crops but rather than sowing between slow-growing crops, you sow quick-growing crops after a main crop has been harvested but before another crop goes in the ground. For example, your plan is to dig up early-grown broad beans in spring and replace them with Brussels sprouts. If the sprouts seedlings aren't yet ready, you can sow and harvest another quick-growing crop while you're waiting for them. The bonus is that you utilize space that might otherwise turn into a weed patch. Fast-growing crops include lettuce, radishes and spinach. Or try green manures such as mustard, phacelia, red clover or lupins. Most will add nitrogen to the soil as well as preventing weeds.

Intercropping

Space-savers This is a good example of catch cropping – fast-growing lettuce planted between slower-growing sweetcorn.

Intercropping partners

Salads, leafy crops and radishes are best for fast-growing intercropping vegetables. Always keep an eye out for space so you can maximize the amount of produce you get from your allotment. Sowing seeds every few weeks will mean you have a regular supply of vegetables. Combined with the use of cloches during cooler periods, intercropping should ensure you have vegetables all year long, with no gaps between harvesting one crop and waiting for the next one to grow. If you still have patches of bare soil, cover them with weed-suppressing fabric to keep them clear.

PARTNERS

- early peas – radishes – autumn turnips
- parsnips (harvested by early spring) – salad leaves – runner beans
- broad beans – spinach – leeks

step 10

sowing & planting

sowing seeds indoors • sowing methods • sowing seeds outside • planting methods • fruit trees & bushes

step 10 Starting plants inside

You will start most plants off by sowing seeds. One exception is garlic, where you plant a clove. The first time you do either of these is exciting and it's a feeling that never wanes, however many years you do it. If you have limited space, don't waste it by sowing seeds that happily germinate outdoors. Instead, use it for tender crops, such as peppers and tomatoes, that need a long growing season.

Sideways on Courgettes, squashes and pumpkin seeds should be sown in spring on their side to stop water sitting on the surface and rotting them.

Garlic cloves Plant these indoors in winter or spring by pushing cloves firmly into the compost, leaving just the tip above the surface. Keep well watered and plant outside in early spring.

Sowing methods

There are various techniques for sowing seeds indoors. Much depends on the size of seed and the container that is used. As a rule of thumb, large seeds, such as cucumbers, broad beans and pumpkins, are sown individually into pots, as they need the space to grow. Medium-sized seeds are often sown into modules, with one or two seeds in each one. Small seeds, such as lettuce and leeks, are often scattered onto a seed tray and pricked out, or moved into individual pots, later. Some pot-sown seeds are potted on – moved to larger pots – before they are planted out. Certain vegetables are nearly always grown directly outdoors as they don't transfer well. The taproots of carrots, for instance, don't like disturbance, while potatoes are too large to be transferred. However, potatoes do benefit from being started indoors first (see Potatoes, p.152), but are then planted directly in the soil.

Peppers are rather tender and need a long growing season, so they need sowing indoors in spring into individual pots. Plant them out in spring after the risk of frost is over.

Chilli seeds are fairly large and will benefit from being sown individually into pots and placed in a propagator at 18°C (64°F). Keep them well watered while they germinate.

French beans love the deep root run provided by toilet-roll tubes and can be sown individually into each "pot". The cardboard tubes will rot when they are planted outdoors.

Indoor sowing

Sowing your seeds indoors enables you to get your crops off to an early start, extends the growing season and prevents seedlings from being destroyed by a harsh frost.

♦ **IDEALLY, SEEDS SHOULD BE SOWN** in a greenhouse or polytunnel. If you don't have either of these, then they can be sown at home and placed on a sunny windowsill. Cheap, heated propagators can be purchased to get your seedlings off to an early start. A temperature of around 12°C (54°F) is required for hardy crops and 18°C (64°F) for the more tender ones.

♦ **DON'T FORGET THAT** plants sown indoors will need hardening off if they are to spend the rest of their days outdoors. Do this by leaving them outside during the day for about a week and bringing them in at night. Alternatively, you can place them in a cold frame for a few days before you plant them in the ground.

How to sow seeds

There are many different techniques for seed sowing. Which one to use depends partly on the size of the seed, but also whether seedlings can cope with root disturbance or close competition from other seedlings growing nearby.

Seeds can also be sown inside or out, although certain crops, particularly root crops such as carrots, radishes, parsnips, turnips and beetroot, should always be sown directly. There are few hard and fast rules; these are just suggestions below, but experiment yourself to see what works best for you. All a seed really needs is soil or compost, light and water.

HOW MANY SEEDS

- **One seed per pot:** broad beans, globe artichokes, celeriac
- **A few seeds per pot:** cauliflowers, Florence fennel, tomatoes, spring onions, onions
- **Two seeds per pot:** French beans, runner beans
- **In a long tube (such as a toilet-roll tube):** sweet peas, peas, mangetout, sweetcorn
- **A few seeds in module trays:** Brussels sprouts, kohl rabi, broccoli
- **In a seed tray:** leeks, cabbage, lettuces, celery (on the surface)
- **On their sides:** courgettes, cucumbers, pumpkins, marrows, squashes
- **In a heated propagator:** chillies, melons, tomatoes, peppers, aubergines

Cabbages have medium-sized seeds and should be sown with one or two seeds per module into seed compost. Thin the seedlings out to one per module once they have germinated.

Brussels sprouts should be sown into modules and then pricked out into larger pots when they have germinated. Firm the soil thoroughly after planting out.

Broad beans can be sown one seed per pot or "growing tube" in late autumn for an early crop the following year. In warmer areas you can sow them directly outdoors in autumn or spring.

Starting plants outside

Most vegetables can be sown directly outdoors, so if you don't have a greenhouse or room on your window ledge to nurse your emerging seedlings under cover, it doesn't matter. You may have to wait until a little later in the year before sowing some of the more tender plants outside – just check the seed packets.

Preparing for seed sowing

Break up the soil in the vegetable bed and add plenty of bulky organic material such as garden compost or well-rotted manure. Dig over the bed, removing any weeds or stones. Then rake over the soil to produce a fine tilth, or fine crumbly soil, because a far finer grade of soil is needed for sowing than for planting. Avoid adding fresh manure or compost if sowing carrots.

Get ready Dig in lots of organic matter and rake it level. Ideally, leave the soil to settle before sowing.

Sowing methods

Small seeds such as carrots, lettuce and parsnips are usually sown thinly in drills, or grooves, in the soil. Drills can be made by using the edge of a hoe along the line created by a string tied tightly between two canes, thus ensuring that the drill is truly straight. Seeds germinate better if the drill is moistened lightly before sowing using a watering can with a rose. Larger seeds are usually sown directly at their final spacing. Often a cluster of seeds can be sown at each spot and thinned out to the strongest seedling. Larger seeds are sown using a dibber, or pointed wooden stick, to create the hole. The seed is placed in the hole, which is then backfilled and watered. Occasionally, seed beds are created by scattering seeds over a prepared area, raking them in and pricking them out later into their final positions. This is often the technique used for sowing leeks. Protect all your seedlings from slugs and snails.

Beans of all types are hungry plants, so add plenty of organic matter prior to sowing. Sow two or three seeds in each hole. Thin the seedlings out to the strongest when they emerge.

Courgettes are usually sown indoors but they can be sown outside after the risk of frosts is over. They like heavy soil, so add lots of organic matter to the ground before sowing.

Pumpkins should be sown with two or three seeds in each hole, thinned out to the strongest after germination. Put plenty of well-rotted manure around each seedling.

Direct sowing

Sowing outdoors, otherwise known as direct sowing, is easy. You can warm the seed bed up first by covering it with plastic sheeting or by placing cloches over it for a few days prior to sowing. This will help to speed up the process of germination. Always have a sheet of fleece or a cloche at the ready later on if it looks as if the emerging seedlings are going to get hit by frost.

◆ **EMERGING SEEDLINGS** often need to be thinned out to the strongest and healthiest specimens. Information about the space you should leave between seedlings when thinning them is provided on the back of the seed packet. Keep the area free from competing weeds and water the plants regularly as they grow. If you wish to continue sowing and harvesting vegetables into autumn and winter, the plants will need to be covered up with cloches to protect them from the cold.

How to sow your seeds outside

Many of the seeds listed below can be sown indoors in trays and pots as well as outdoors. This is a general guide; some varieties are dwarfing or more vigorous, so adjust their spacing accordingly. Nor are the distances given final, as many seeds are later thinned out. Always check planting distances on the back of seed packets and if in doubt, ask an experienced gardener. A bonus of working on your vegetable plot is that your neighbours will be able to offer friendly advice and you can benefit from their experience.

- **Sow thinly in a drill:** broccoli, Brussels sprouts, cabbages, cauliflowers, kale, beetroot, carrots, turnips, spinach, swedes, lettuces, radishes
- **Sow 10cm (4in) apart:** garlic sets, onion sets
- **Sow 15cm (6in) apart:** runner beans, French beans
- **Sow 30–38cm (12–15in) apart:** perpetual spinach
- **Plant in blocks:** leeks, sweetcorn
- **Plant in a flat drill:** peas 5–7cm (2–2¾in) apart in staggered rows, Swiss chard
- **Plant in staggered rows 23cm (9in) apart:** broad beans
- **Plant in a seed bed for transplanting later:** leeks (thinly) in drills 15cm (6in) apart and 1cm (¼in) deep
- **Sow two seeds together 90cm (3ft) apart:** courgettes, marrows
- **Sow two seeds together 1.5m (5ft) apart:** pumpkins, squashes
- **Tubers:** potatoes (early) 30cm (12in) apart, potatoes (maincrop) 40–75cm (16–30in), Jerusalem artichokes 90cm (3ft) apart

Cabbages should be sown thinly and thinned regularly as they grow to a final spacing of about 30–45cm (12–18in). If the soil is acidic, it should have lime added to it first.

Lettuces should be sown thinly in shallow drills. They can be harvested as young leaves or thinned out to make bigger plants. Sow seeds fortnightly for crops through the season.

Potatoes are planted in spring into rows of trenches, then covered with soil enriched with organic matter. Gently earth the soil up as the young plant shoots emerge.

Planting methods

Sweetcorn Being a wind-pollinated plant, sweetcorn should be planted not in rows, but in a grid pattern to aid pollination.

"use a wooden **board** to walk on **veg** beds"

There are many different techniques for planting your crops. It all depends on whether you are planting out your seedlings or planting young fruit trees and bushes. Whichever it is, your two main requirements are well-prepared soil and regular watering after planting.

Planting vegetable seedlings

You can either grow seedlings yourself or buy them at your local garden centre. Although it is more expensive to buy ready-grown plants, it is a useful time-saver if you haven't had a chance to grow everything you want from seed. Always check the labels on packets of seeds and plants, as planting requirements – and especially the recommended distances between plants – vary for each type of vegetable. Even within a group of plants such as cabbages, the distance between each one can range from 30cm (12in) for compact types to 45cm (18in) for larger varieties. When you are planting out, use a wooden board to walk over the vegetable beds to prevent your boots or shoes compacting the soil.

Planting methods

Top-heavy plants such as Brussels sprouts and sweetcorn benefit from having the soil firmed around their roots to stop them blowing over in the wind. Certain other plants such as leeks shouldn't be firmed in at all; this leaves room for their stems to expand and whiten. If planting in rows, use string tied between two canes to ensure you plant in straight lines. Most vegetables should be planted with the top of their roots flush with the soil.

Cabbages These should be planted firmly into rich, fertile soil. Always check the label for planting distances.

Leeks These are planted differently to most other crops. Use a large dibber, or pointed wooden stick, to create a hole and pop the seedling into it. Don't firm down the soil around it, but instead water it in, leaving the soil to crumble back around the leek.

Keep weeds at bay After planting a fruit tree, suppress weeds by applying weed-control fabric or a layer of mulch around the roots.

Planting fruit trees & bushes

When planting young trees, attach them to a stake to help them grow straight and prevent them from being blown over. Put the stake in the soil before the tree to prevent damage to the roots. Alternatively, use a diagonal stake at 45 degrees.

◆ **USE A TREE GUARD** around the trunk if rabbits are a problem.

◆ **FRUIT TREES** grown on dwarf rootstocks (the rootstock is the lower trunk and roots, onto which a tree is grafted – it can dictate tree size and disease-resistance) are a good choice. Such trees will not grow too big, will not create excessive shade and their roots will not grow into your veg beds.

◆ **BARE-ROOT FRUIT TREES** are usually available from late autumn through to late winter. They are often cheaper and healthier than container-grown trees. Bare-root trees should be planted while still dormant; container trees can be planted at any time of year.

Containers

Fruit trees and bushes can be grown in containers. This is ideal if the soil on the allotment is poor. It also restricts the size of the tree, preventing it from getting too big for the plot. Choose dwarf varieties of fruit trees for pots and containers.

Compost and fertilizer Ensure the container has adequate drainage and use a mix of compost and fertilizer.

Level of soil Plant the tree at the same depth as it was in its pot and firm it in well. Mulch the surface with compost.

Planting depths

Do not plant fruit trees too deeply as this can quickly rot the trunk. Most trees have a graft union low down on the trunk, where the tree has been grafted onto a rootstock (see left). The graft union should always remain above the soil.

Apple Place a stick across the hole to check the tree is at the same level as it was in its pot. Backfill with quality compost.

Blackcurrants Blackcurrants are an exception; plant them about 5cm (2in) deeper than they were in their pot.

Raspberries These are planted out as individual canes. Plant them to the same depth as the soil mark on the canes.

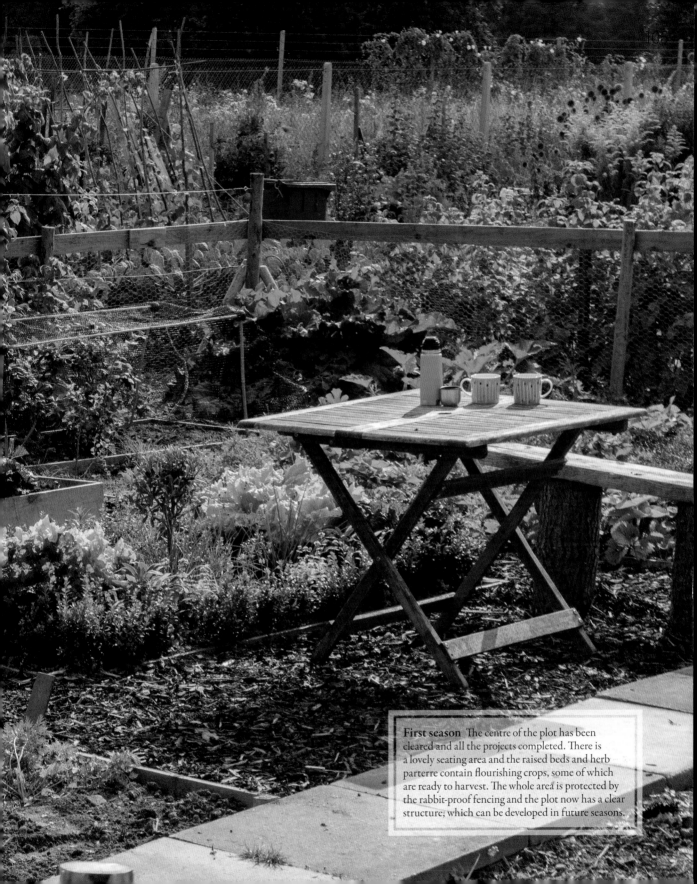

First season The centre of the plot has been cleared and all the projects completed. There is a lovely seating area and the raised beds and herb parterre contain flourishing crops, some of which are ready to harvest. The whole area is protected by the rabbit-proof fencing and the plot now has a clear structure, which can be developed in future seasons.

VEG
Growing & Storing

vegetables

leafy crops

cabbages & oriental brassicas • Brussels sprouts • spinach & chard • lettuce & salad leaves • chicory & endive • kale

Cabbages & Oriental brassicas

Not only are cabbages healthy and surprisingly tasty, but they also have a wonderful ornamental quality to them, coming in a wide range of shapes and colours and adding interest and texture to the allotment plot. But the main reason they are so useful is that they will provide a bumper crop all year round.

Netting Net cabbages to protect them from cabbage white butterflies and pigeons.

Sowing

Sow cabbage seeds from early spring to late summer, depending on their group (see right). You can either sow them under cover in small plastic pots or in a seed bed.

Transplanting When the plants are 6cm (2½in) high, transplant them to their final position, leaving 30–45cm (12–18in) between each plant.

Growing

Cabbages fall into three groups – spring, summer and winter, depending on when they are to be harvested. Spring cabbages are sown in July and August and transplanted in September/October. Summer cabbages are sown from early March until early May and transplanted in May/June. Winter cabbages are sown in April/May, then transplanted in late June/July. Firm transplanted cabbages in well to stop the wind from rocking them.

◆ **CABBAGES REQUIRE** a sunny, sheltered position in rich, fertile but well-drained soil. Dig in organic matter such as well-rotted manure before planting. If your soil is poor, consider building raised beds and filling them with a mix of good-quality soil, compost and manure. Avoid growing cabbages in the same ground as the previous year as they are prone to soil-borne diseases such as clubroot. Instead, practise crop rotation.

savoy

'Prospera'

pointed cabbage

Oriental greens

These late-summer vegetables can be either eaten raw, added to stir-fries, or cooked like traditional cabbage. They require a fertile soil in full sun. Sow seeds in drills 1cm (½in) deep in rows 38cm (15in) apart. Thin seedlings to 15cm (6in) apart for cut-and-come-again salad leaves or 30cm (12in) apart for large heads.

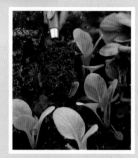

Mulching Regularly water and mulch Chinese lettuce to prevent plants from bolting.

Cut leaves Harvest succulent young leaves with scissors as a cut-and-come-again crop.

Harvest whole Alternatively, leave plants to form large heads and harvest at the end of summer.

Routine care

Cabbages are hungry plants so give them a liquid feed every couple of weeks to keep them lush and healthy. Water them daily during dry periods and weed around the plants regularly to prevent them having to compete with the weeds for nutrients.

◆ **WATCH OUT** for pests and diseases. The worst culprits are pigeons – these will tear cabbages to shreds, so cover the cabbages with a net. Cabbage white butterfly and cabbage root fly are the other pests to watch out for (see p.127).

Harvesting Spring cabbages are ready to harvest during April and May, summer cabbages between July and September and autumn and winter cabbages from September onwards.

Storing & Using

Cabbage can be used for: salads...stir-fries...soups... sauerkraut...casseroles...

Cabbages can remain in the ground for longer than many other vegetables so you can largely cut them and use them as and when you want. If you want to store them, the traditional method is in a net in a cool, dry garage or cellar.

Sauerkraut This traditional dish uses very finely shredded cabbage that has been pickled or fermented. It will keep for many months.

red cabbage

Chinese broccoli

pak choi

mizuna

Brussels sprouts

Although not to everybody's taste, Brussels sprouts are rich in vitamin C, and there are lots of tasty ways of cooking them to give them wider appeal. A useful crop for winter, new varieties have been bred for extra sweetness, and there are also exciting red-leaved varieties to try.

Sowing outdoors

Sprouts can either be sown under cover and then planted out as seedlings (see below), or sown directly into the soil in spring.

♦ **IF SOWING** directly into the ground, the soil should be thoroughly dug over and all weeds removed. Like other members of the cabbage family, sprouts prefer a heavy, rich soil, so add lots of organic matter, such as well-rotted manure. Rake the soil level then leave it to settle for a couple of weeks before sowing.

♦ **SOW SEED** in mid-spring. Use the edge of a draw hoe to create a shallow 1cm (½in) drill, or narrow trench, in the soil and sow thinly in rows 15cm (6in) apart. When the seedlings emerge they should be thinned out to 7.5cm (3in).

Acquired taste Brussels sprouts are sweet and tender when young, and become even sweeter and more delicious once they have been touched by frost a few times.

Sowing indoors

Seeds can be sown indoors in late winter for an early crop in late summer. Fill module trays with good-quality seed compost and water well. Use a dibber to make a 2cm (¾in) hole in each module and sow two seeds. Water again and then leave to germinate. Thin out to leave the strongest seedling in each module. As with all seedlings, harden them off for 7–10 days before planting outside.

Strongest seedlings Select the strongest and healthiest sprouts to plant out when they have reached 10cm (4in) high.

Planting distance Seedlings should be planted 60cm (24in) apart. Firm them in well after planting and water thoroughly.

Brassica collar Sprouts are prone to damage by cabbage root fly. Place brassica collars at the base of the stems to deter them.

Routine care

Keep the plants well watered during dry periods, and mulch around the base of the plants with well-rotted manure to retain moisture. Sprouts are tall plants and may need support using canes and string in exposed, windy sites.

◆ **MOST OLDER** varieties ripen upwards from the bottom of the stem. Newer varieties develop at a more equal rate and can be cut as whole stems once all the sprouts reach a good size.

◆ **SPROUTS CAN** either be removed from the stem with a sharp knife or twisted off with your fingers. Harvest as and when they are needed as they don't keep for long after picking.

Harvesting Brussels sprouts sown in spring are ready for harvesting from winter to spring. Plants sown indoors in winter will be ready to harvest in late summer.

Growing tips

Sprouts are easy to grow but it is important to watch out for some of the main pests that all members of the cabbage family are prone to, such as cabbage root fly, birds, and cabbage white butterflies.

Netting Cover plants with netting to prevent the crop from being damaged by birds. Pigeons are particularly fond of the leaves of brassicas, such as sprouts.

Earthing up Prevent these top-heavy vegetables from toppling in the wind by earthing soil up around the base of each plant for extra stability.

Good practice Remove the ageing yellow leaves as the plant matures to improve air circulation and prevent the sprouts from rotting.

Storing & Using

They can be used in: soups...mashes...stir-fries...bubble & squeak...or frozen...

Sprouts are best picked as you need them. They can also be kept in a fridge for a week, or blanch them and keep in a freezer for about 12 months. Brussels sprouts mean Christmas dinner to many people, but they can be used in many ways. Their flavour goes so well with many things: blue cheese, chestnuts, smoked bacon or crème fraîche. Tossed with butter and Parmesan cheese, they make a tasty side dish.

Sprout tops These bushy leaves at the top of the stalk are less pungent than sprouts but extremely tender, and can be used like kale or cabbage.

sprouts

Spinach & Chard

Fresh spinach leaves are so tasty and healthy to eat that it's no wonder Popeye was such a devotee. They can be regularly harvested while young and used in salads, or left to mature for cooking. Chard leaves are also delicious, with the bonus that they add a splash of colour to the allotment, with their vivid stems.

Frost protection Protect early-sown crops with a cloche, but remove for a time on warm days.

Sowing

Sow chard in mid-spring. Make a 2.5cm (1in) drill and sow seeds about 7.5cm (3in) apart, in rows spaced at 38cm (15in). Water the rows well and label the plants.

Sow seeds individually Sow spinach seeds 2.5cm (1in) apart from early spring to early summer, in drills 1cm (½in) deep. Cover over with soil and water thoroughly.

Thinning Seedlings can be thinned out when they are 2cm (¾in) tall. Chard should be thinned to 30cm (12in) apart, spinach to 20cm (8in) apart.

Growing

Both spinach and chard prefer a sunny or slightly shaded location in moist but free-draining soil. Both are easy to grow, although they have slightly different sowing and harvesting times.

◆ **CHARD SHOULD** be sown mainly in springtime, directly into the soil, which will give a regular crop of attractive leaves during the summer months. It is possible to extend the season through to autumn or winter with later sowings and by keeping the plants protected under cloches.

◆ **SPINACH IS** either sown outside in spring and harvested in summer, or sown in late summer and harvested in autumn. In order to guarantee a constant supply of spinach you can sow seed every two to three weeks.

spinach

white chard

Routine care

Both spinach and chard require relatively little upkeep once sown and thinned. Look out for mildew on spinach and remove affected leaves. Choose varieties that offer disease resistance. Keep the seedlings free of weeds and water the plants regularly during dry spells. Give the plants a high-nitrogen liquid feed every couple of weeks to keep them green and productive.

◆ **IF YOU WISH** to grow spinach as a cut-and-come-again crop, don't thin out the seedlings and harvest the leaves regularly.

Harvesting

Spring sowings of chard are ready for harvesting about 12 weeks after sowing, while spinach can be cut after 8–12 weeks. Crop sooner if growing them as cut-and-come-again.

Young shoots Regularly pick over the plants to ensure that new fresh growth is produced. Leaves can be harvested young, as soon as they are large enough, or left to reach full size. Take care not to damage the main growing point in the centre.

Bolting Keep chard plants well watered during summer to prevent them from flowering, or "bolting", which spoils the crop. Spinach has a tendency to bolt, particularly in hot, dry weather. Choose resistant varieties or grow in light shade.

Storing & Using

They can be made into: soups...salads...casseroles ...pies...or frozen...

Spinach and chard leaves taste best when picked young and fresh, and can be added to salads. Brightly coloured chard stems are also edible and can be used in a range of dishes. Spinach and chard can both be frozen. Blanch first by boiling for a couple of minutes, cooling in iced water, then drying on a tea towel. Once defrosted both are best cooked rather than eaten raw or in salads.

Harvesting all If preferred, you can harvest whole plants at once, leaving room for others nearby to develop.

rhubarb chard

rainbow chard

red chard

Lettuce & Salad leaves

Lettuce is often the main ingredient used in salads, and the range of varieties is vast. However, it is only one of many leafy salad crops, which include tasty rocket, sorrel, and lamb's lettuce. Salad leaves are quick and easy to grow, which also makes them perfect "fillers" for squeezing in between slower growing crops, such as turnips. With a bit of planning and cold protection, it is possible to be harvesting salad leaves all year.

Sowing outdoors

Salad leaves can be sown outdoors in drills from early spring to late summer. Dig over the soil, removing any weeds, before raking the area so the surface is level.

Make a drill Draw out a drill about 1cm (½in) deep and then lightly sow the seeds, cover them over with soil, and then water them lightly.

Thinning out Plants grown for mature, full-size heads should be thinned out to about 25cm (10in) apart. Don't thin cut-and-come-again crops.

Growing

There are basically four types of lettuce. Cos types are upright with loose hearts. Crispheads have tightly folded, crunchy leaves, and a solid heart, such as iceberg. Butterheads have soft, folded leaves with round hearts. Finally, there are the looseleaf types, which can be grown as cut-and-come-again. Lettuce prefers light, well-drained soil, and will tolerate some light shade. They are a good choice for growing in containers if kept well watered.

◆ **SEEDS CAN BE** sown directly in the soil (see left), or for an earlier crop, they can also be sown in late winter under cover and planted out when the risk of frost has passed.

◆ **WHEN SOWING UNDER COVER,** sow two or three seeds into small pots of compost. Thin to leave the strongest seedling.

◆ **KEEP PLANTS** well watered during dry periods, as this will help prevent "bolting" or running to seed. Regularly weed among the growing plants to prevent any competition for nutrients.

'Little Gem' 'Tom Thumb' 'Lollo Rosso'

Protection

Slugs and snails can swiftly devastate a healthy crop of salad leaves, particularly during wet weather. Protect plants by laying grit or sharp sand around them, or lightly sprinkle slug pellets around the area. Aphids also enjoy feeding on leaves, so check over the plants regularly.

Grit Sprinkle grit or sharp sand around the plants as slugs hate the coarse, dry texture.

Netting If birds are a problem on your allotment, cover lettuce plants with a net to protect them.

Plastic bottles Use plastic bottles to protect leaves from slugs. They also act as mini cloches.

Harvesting

Cut-and-come-again crops are simply cut just above the base of the plants using scissors once the leaves are large enough. They will then resprout, ready to crop again in a few days if watered well. Cut regularly to prevent the leaves getting too big and leggy.

◆ **HEARTING TYPES**, those that form heads, should be cut just above the soil using a sharp knife.

◆ **LOOSELEAF VARIETIES** are best harvested only when required, as they soon wilt. The cut leaves will keep in a fridge for a day or two.

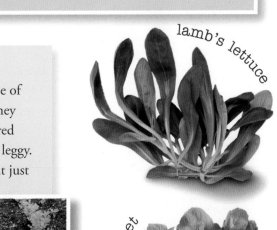

Pick again Pick and sow seeds frequently for a regular supply of lettuce for your salad bowl.

lamb's lettuce

rocket

Batavia

romaine

sorrel

Chinese

Chicory & Endive

These crops are grown in a similar way to lettuce, although they are hardier and can be cropped well into autumn. There are three types of chicory: sugar loaf, red-leaved (or radicchio) and Witloof. There are also two different types of endive, curly-leaved varieties and Batavian-types, which have broad leaves.

Batavian endive

Sowing

Chicory and endive can be sown indoors for a head start, or outside a few weeks later. Wait until the soil has started to warm if sowing outside to prevent the plants bolting.

Sowing seeds Dig over the site, remove any weeds and sow thinly into drills, 1cm (½in) deep.

Watering Thin seedlings out to 30cm (12in) apart and keep them well watered throughout summer.

Witloof chicory

Growing

Chicory and endive require rich, well-drained soil, and will grow in sun or light shade. Winter crops can be grown under cover or in cloches.

◆ **SOW SEEDS** indoors in early spring into trays; directly outside from mid-spring.

◆ **PLANTS SHOULD** be kept well watered during summer to prevent them from bolting.

◆ **ENDIVES CAN** be blanched to reduce bitterness. Tie the leaves together, place a pot over them and harvest after 15 days.

◆ **PICK WHEN** leaves have reached a suitable size. Baby leaves can also be harvested as cut-and-come-again salad leaves.

curly endive

"Chicons" Witloof chicory is often forced to produce "chicons", or fleshy shoots, in winter. Plant mature roots into pots in autumn and keep them dark. Harvest the shoots when 10cm (4in) tall.

radicchio

Kale

These vitamin-rich plants are one of the most ornamental and architectural members of the cabbage family, with a range of different shapes, heights and colours, including varieties with crinkly and curly leaves and coloured foliage.

Growing

Kale requires rich, fertile but well-drained soil, and plenty of space, although dwarf varieties are available. Young plants are planted out or transplanted in early summer into their final positions. Stake taller varieties to prevent them blowing over.

◆ **PROTECT KALE** from cabbage root fly by placing collars around the base of each plant. Cover with a fine-meshed net to prevent cabbage white butterflies and pigeons attacking them.

◆ **LEAVES CAN** be harvested throughout autumn and winter by picking them individually. Dispose of the plants when they flower the following spring.

Harvesting Harvest the tender inner leaves every few days. The outer leaves are coarser and less tasty.

Storing & Using

It can be used in: pies... soups...or can be frozen...

Kale goes well with fish and meat, and is commonly boiled or steamed to accompany the Sunday roast. It can also be used in stir-fries, casseroles, and pasta dishes. Store the leaves in a fridge for up to a week or freeze them for up to 9 months.

Pie Using either shortcrust or filo pastry, kale can be combined with cheese, onions and eggs to make a tasty pie.

Sowing

Seeds can be sown 1cm (½in) deep into pots under cover in spring, or directly into drills outside from mid-spring. Plants raised outside are transplanted into their final positions once large enough.

Indoor seedlings Seedlings raised indoors should be grown on until large enough to plant outside in their final positions. Repot them as required.

Planting distance Plants should be planted out, spaced 45cm (18in) apart. Keep them well watered and support taller varieties as they grow.

purple kale

green kale

vegetables
fruiting & flowering

tomatoes • cucumbers & aubergines • broccoli & cauliflowers • courgettes & marrows • pumpkins • squashes • peppers & chillies • sweetcorn • globe artichokes

Tomatoes

Tomatoes are very easy to grow, either under cover or outside in a sunny position, and produce a reliable harvest from midsummer. There are many varieties to choose from, producing fruit in a wide range of colours, flavours, and sizes. These fall into two types: cordon tomatoes that are usually trained up tall canes or strings, and bush varieties that are grown untrained.

Growing bags

Growing bags can be used on a veg plot, and allow you to easily give tomatoes the sunny, sheltered site they require.

Make a hole The planting holes in your growing bag should be large enough to plant the tomatoes into and to allow easy watering. Remember to make drainage holes in the base.

Keep watered Tomato plants are particularly thirsty when they are in flower or fruit. The compost in the growing bags needs to be kept moist.

Growing

Sow tomato seeds under cover in early spring. Fill a pot or tray with compost, water well, and sow the seeds on top, spacing them 1cm (½in) apart. Lightly cover with compost and place in a propagator or on a warm windowsill.

◆ **WHEN THE** seedlings have their first pair of leaves, prick them out into individual pots and grow under cover until the risk of frost has passed. Repot them into larger pots as necessary.

◆ **PLANT OUT** about 30cm (12in) apart, or three per growing bag, in a sheltered but sunny spot. Insert tall canes near each plant for support – one per cordon variety, four per bush tomato.

◆ **IMPROVE THE SOIL** before planting tomatoes out with some well-rotted manure mixed into the soil to give the plants a good start. This also helps to stop the plants drying out.

yellow cherry

cherry plum

plum

salad

beefsteak

red cherry

Routine care

If you look after tomatoes properly and give them the right growing conditions, they will reward you with a good, steady crop from about July to September or even October.

◆ **IT IS IMPORTANT** to keep plants well watered, as drying out will affect their growth and may cause damage to the developing fruits. Use a tomato feed weekly once flowers appear.

◆ **CORDON** tomatoes are grown as single stems up a cane or string support. Tie them in with soft twine as they grow. Once cordon plants have formed four or five trusses of flowers, cut out the top of the plants to stop further growth.

◆ **TOMATOES** ripen from midsummer onwards. For the best flavour, wait until each fruit is evenly coloured. Smaller tomatoes ripen quickly in good weather but larger fruits, such as beefsteak-types, can take several days to ripen completely.

Growing tips

Water all plants regularly, even as much as once a day in very hot weather, and feed them using a high-potash tomato fertilizer. Avoid letting plants dry out, which can cause the fruit to split, and may lead to the nutrient disorder, blossom end rot (see p.235). If growing tomatoes in a greenhouse, ensure plants are well ventilated.

Support Tie in the stems of cordon tomatoes to give them support, as they become heavy with the growing fruit.

Pinch out The sideshoots of cordon tomatoes should be pinched out regularly, but leave those on bush tomatoes to grow. Pinch out carefully with your fingers, supporting the stem with the other hand.

Storing & Using

They can be used for: ketchup...chutney... soups...sauces...or can be chilled...or oven-dried...

Tomatoes keep well in the fridge for a few days but they cannot be frozen. Gluts can also be oven-dried, or preserved in a wide range of dishes, such as green tomato chutney or tomato ketchup, or in stocks and soup bases that can be frozen.

Oven-dried tomatoes Useful in many dishes, pack them into sterilized jars and cover with olive oil. They will keep for up to 6 months stored in a cool, dark cupboard.

Sauce Making tomato ketchup is great fun and you know exactly what ingredients are in it. It will keep for around 6 months in sterilized bottles, and goes just as well with steak and chips, as it does with bangers and mash.

Chutney Tomatoes really lend themselves to chutney and you can use either ripe or green tomatoes. Green tomatoes are good to use at the end of the season. Chutney will keep for 6 to 12 months in a cupboard.

black cherry grape

Cucumbers

Fresh salads wouldn't be the same without cucumber. It is a summer essential. Containing next to no calories and cool, refreshing and healthy, this member of the cucurbit family is a must for the veggie plot. If you don't have a greenhouse, then the most suitable type for growing outdoors is the ridge cucumber.

Growing

Cucumbers should be sown in early spring as they require a long growing season to ripen their fruit. However, be aware that they don't like fluctuations in temperature during the early stages of germination, so ensure they have constant warmth to begin with. Start them off indoors, sowing one seed per 10cm (4in) pot and placing the pots in a propagator. Once they have germinated, keep them under cover until there is no longer any danger of frost.

♦ **OUTDOOR VARIETIES** have male and female flowers and you may need to help with pollination for them to produce fruit. Do this by simply picking a male flower and pushing it into the female flowers.

♦ **MANY INDOOR VARIETIES** only produce female flowers and do not require pollination. If they are pollinated, the cucumbers will be bitter.

Protection Use cloches to protect the young plants from frosts. Cloches will also help to speed up fruiting.

Growing tips

If you have enough room, cucumbers can be left to scramble and sprawl over the ground. However, if space is at a premium, consider growing them up bamboo canes or up a purpose-built frame.

Frame Whether you use a purpose-built frame or construct your own using bamboo canes, you must tie your growing cucumber plants to it securely.

Harvesting Harvest cucumbers regularly using secateurs. This encourages the plant to crop more and the younger cucumbers will taste better.

ridge cucumber

cucumber

Storing & Using
They can be: pickled...

Eat cucumbers as soon as possible as they aren't suitable for refrigerating for long or for freezing. If you have a glut, pick them small and pickle them in vinegar with dill and spices. They will keep for 6 months.

Aubergines

Aubergines, or egg plants, are trickier to grow than some vegetables but are well worth the effort. To grow them successfully, you need a greenhouse or a sunny, sheltered spot. Get the conditions right and you will be rewarded with five or six of these quirky-looking vegetables per plant.

'Black Beauty'

'Calliope'

'Thai Green'

'Mohican'

Growing

Fill small plastic pots with seed compost in early spring and sow one seed in each. Water them well and place in a heated propagator. Once the seedlings are 6cm (2½in) tall, remove them from the propagator and place them in the greenhouse or on a windowsill to grow them on.

Potting on Plants grown indoors will need potting on. Take care not to disturb the root ball when you do so.

◆ **TO GROW PLANTS OUTDOORS,** first harden the young plants off in a cold frame. Once the risk of frosts is over, plant them out in a warm, sheltered position.

◆ **PICK REGULARLY** to encourage more fruiting and use quickly as aubergines don't keep well. Don't leave the fruit on the plant too long: when you pick them, the aubergines should be nice and shiny. If they have become dull, it is because they are over-ripe.

Growing tips

When the main shoot reaches about 30cm (12in) high, cut it off or pinch it out to encourage the development of side shoots. Water plants regularly and give a liquid feed once a week to keep them healthy. Aubergines become heavy as they swell, so support the stems with canes and string.

Support Use soft twine twisted in a figure-of-eight around the plant and the cane to provide gentle support for the stem.

Storing & Using

Aubergines can be made into: moussaka...ratatouille...

They can only be refrigerated for a few days and can't be frozen, so use them in dishes that can be frozen, such as moussaka.

Broccoli & Cauliflowers

These must be two of the most popular and tasty vegetables from the cabbage family. There are three different types of broccoli: purple and white sprouting, and the more common, large, green-headed broccoli, known as calabrese. New cauliflower varieties come in exciting colours such as orange, purple, and yellow, and offer gardeners the possibility of harvesting tasty, firm heads all year round.

Sowing outdoors

Sow calabrese and spring cauliflowers into 1cm (½in) deep drills, cover with soil, and water gently. Sow calabrese in mid-spring; spring cauliflowers in autumn.

Thinning As the plants develop, thin them to their final spacing. Leave 40cm (16in) between each calabrese; thin spring cauliflowers to 70cm (28in) apart.

Growing

Cauliflowers and broccoli prefer rich, fertile soil, so dig in plenty of well-rotted manure. Prepare the soil thoroughly before sowing or planting, by digging it over and removing any perennial weeds. Calabrese resent root disturbance, so are sown directly in the soil in mid-spring (see left); cauliflowers to harvest in spring are also sown this way during autumn. To give summer cauliflowers a head start, sow them under cover in early spring. Fill small pots with compost, sow two seeds in each, 1cm (½in) deep, then thin out the seedlings to leave the strongest per pot.

◆ **PLANT OUT** the summer cauliflowers when they are about 15cm (6in) tall; they will benefit from being hardened off in a cold frame before you plant them out.

◆ **SUMMER VARIETIES** should be planted at 60cm (24in) apart. Water them well after planting.

broccoli

purple sprouting

broccoli 'Romanesco'

Protection

As the plants grow, keep the soil free from weeds to avoid competition for nutrients. Also keep well watered to prevent the development of fungal diseases such as mildew. The main pests to look out for are birds, particularly pigeons, as they can strip leaves; also be vigilant against cabbage root fly and the caterpillar of the cabbage white butterfly.

Root flies Place a collar at the base of each plant to prevent cabbage root fly laying eggs there.

Pests Cover plants with a net to prevent birds destroying the crop or butterflies laying their eggs on it.

Sun Tie the leaves together to prevent white-headed cauliflowers turning yellow in the sun.

Harvesting

Calabrese are ready from midsummer to mid autumn. They should be harvested when the flower heads have developed but just before they actually open. Harvest the central stem first, which will then allow side shoots to develop for picking later. Purple- and white-sprouting broccoli should be regularly picked: that way their season will extend well into autumn. To spread your cauliflower harvest, start cutting when some of them are young.

◆ **DO NOT LEAVE** cauliflowers too long before harvesting as the florets separate and will taste less good.

cauliflower 'Mayflower'

cauliflower 'Violet Queen'

Storing & Using

They can be used for: salads...soups...gratins... relishes...and frozen...

Cauliflowers can be stored for up to three weeks if you harvest them with their root intact and leave them in a cool, dry place such as a shed. You cannot keep broccoli or calabrese in the fridge for longer than a week. However, if you are faced with a glut, the florets of all these vegetables are suitable for freezing. Be sure to blanch them first to preserve their texture and flavour. They will keep for up to a year.

Piccalilli This crunchy relish includes cauliflower florets and gets its lovely bright yellow colour from mustard and turmeric. Keeps for up to 6 months.

Courgettes & Marrows

Just one or two plants will reward you with bumper crops throughout the summer, so make sure you allocate some space for these essential and nutritious veggies. Although you can grow specific marrow varieties, if you leave courgettes on the plant for long enough, they will rapidly become as big as marrows.

Pollination Tie up the female flower for up to a day after pollination.

Sowing

Courgettes and marrows are easy to grow. Seeds should be sown indoors in mid- to late-spring. Sow one seed per pot, 3cm (1¼in) deep in general-purpose compost.

Sideways Lay the seed on its side to prevent it from rotting in the compost before it has a chance to germinate.

Outdoors Seeds can be sown outdoors when there is no more risk of frost. Use a dibber and plant two seeds per hole, 3cm (1¼in) deep and 90cm (36in) apart. Thin to one seedling per hole when they emerge.

Growing

Wait until the risk of frost is over before planting out the seedlings. If they have outgrown their pots, they may need potting on into something bigger if the weather conditions are still unsuitable for growing outside. While keeping them indoors, water every few days and give them a liquid feed fortnightly to keep them strong and healthy.

◆ **PREPARE THE** ground a few weeks before planting out, to give the soil time to settle. Thoroughly dig the soil over and incorporate plenty of well-rotted manure or compost: courgettes and marrows require a rich, fertile soil to help them cope with their tendency to produce heavy crops.

◆ **USE A TROWEL** to make the planting hole and place them out at 90cm (36in) apart. Water them in thoroughly.

round varieties

courgette & flower

Protection

Young seedlings are vulnerable to slugs and snails when they are first planted in the soil, particularly if it has been a damp spring. To combat these pests, lightly sprinkle slug pellets around the area. Alternatively, you can set beer traps or place sharp sand or grit around individual plants. A sprinkling of bran also helps to deter slugs.

Glass panels Place panels of glass around individual plants for the first few days to protect the leaves against cool spring evenings.

Cloches If sowing directly, the soil can be warmed up beforehand by erecting cloches for a few days prior to planting.

Plastic bottles Use old plastic bottles to create mini cloches for seedlings when they are still vulnerable to late-spring frosts.

Routine care

Watch out for powdery mildew. Keeping the roots well watered should help prevent it spreading too quickly. Remove infected leaves as soon as they appear.

◆ **HARVEST** courgettes with secateurs or a knife when they reach about 12cm (5in) long. They need to be picked regularly to keep them cropping. If you want marrows, leave some to develop further.

Watering If you can't manage to water your plants every day, plunge an upside-down bottle with its end cut off and filled with water into the soil next to the plant. This will keep it watered for a few days.

Storing & Using

They can be used for: stuffing...soups...stews... cakes & muffins...fritters...salads...or frozen...

As well as harvesting courgettes and marrows and eating them straight away, you can also use the large, yellow trumpet-like flowers of courgettes to make fritters. Courgettes and marrows can be frozen (they will keep for about 6 months) but they aren't as tasty once they have been defrosted, so use the defrosted vegetables in delicious soups and sauces, which you can then freeze and use whenever you please.

Muffins Surprisingly, courgettes and marrows can also successfully be made into delicious muffins and cakes, which bear a resemblance to carrot cake.

marrow 'Tiger Cross'

Pumpkins

Pumpkins are greedy plants and produce their lush foliage and attractive fruit in a rich, heavy soil. If you have poor, infertile soil then you could try growing one on top of the compost heap. Available in a huge variety of shapes, sizes and colours, pumpkins will make an attractive addition to your allotment.

Growing

Seeds should be sown indoors between mid-April and mid-May, which will give the seedlings a chance to get established before you plant them outside. Fill a 7cm (3in) pot with good-quality seed compost and sow one seed per pot – with the seed on its side to prevent it rotting – at a depth of 2.5cm (1in). Put the pot in a greenhouse, propagator or on a light windowsill.

◆ **WHEN THE ROOTS** begin to show through the bottom of the pots, transfer the seedlings into 12cm (5in) pots.

pumpkin

Hardening off Before planting out, the seedlings should be hardened off in a cold frame for a few days.

Planting out

Choose a sunny, sheltered spot and dig in plenty of well-rotted manure or compost to improve the soil before planting your seedlings. Position each on a slightly raised mound of earth at a spacing of 1–2m (3–6ft) to give them room to ramble. Firm the seedlings in and water thoroughly. Mulch around each plant after watering in.

Dig a hole Create a hole large enough for the rootball, then slide the seedling out of its pot.

Firm in Firm the seedling in and mulch around it with well-rotted manure.

Regular feeding Pumpkins need feeding regularly; if their leaves start to turn yellow, it's a sign that they need to be fed.

Routine care

◆ **FEED PLANTS** weekly with a general-purpose liquid fertilizer or tomato feed. The potash in the feed will develop their colour, size and flavour.

◆ **PLACE A** thick layer of mulch around each plant to conserve moisture and suppress weeds.

◆ **REMOVE SOME** of the fruitlets before they get too big, leaving just two or three on the plant so that it puts its energy into producing larger fruit.

◆ **KEEP THE AREA** around young plants well weeded to avoid them having to compete with weeds for nutrients and water.

◆ **THE FRUITS** are ready to harvest from late September to early November. When the stems crack and the skin hardens, it means that the fruits are ready. If possible, leave them to dry in the autumn sun for a week or two, then, before the first frosts, cut them off, leaving a length of stalk attached to prevent rotting.

Large specimens

If you want really big fruits, choose large varieties. Remove most of the fruitlets, leaving just two or three on each plant. Feed weekly and you should get prize-size pumpkins.

Stop the rot Place large pumpkins on bricks, tiles or blocks of wood to prevent them rotting into the soil.

Storing & Using

They can be used in: soups...curries... casseroles...pies...ravioli...risottos... bread...or roasted...or frozen...

Pumpkins store extremely well if they are properly "cured", which means letting their skins harden fully in the sun for 10 days or so after harvesting. Store them for up to 6 months in a cool, dry place. You can also purée or boil the peeled pumpkin, divide it into portions and freeze for up to 6 months.

Pumpkin butter This delicious sweet spread is made by cooking pumpkin with apple juice and spices. It will keep in the fridge for up to 6 months.

Pumpkin pie Traditionally eaten in the United States at Thanksgiving, this dessert is made using the flesh of the pumpkin, eggs, milk, sugar and spices.

Pumpkin seeds Roast these in the oven on a baking tray, drizzled with a little olive oil and sprinkled with chilli flakes. The result will be a healthy, tasty snack.

Halloween

The most recognizable symbol of Halloween is a pumpkin carved into a Jack-o'-lantern. Children love them, and what could be more fun than to carve your own home-grown pumpkin? Search the internet for unusual ideas for carving elaborate designs, but if that's not for you, just use a sharp knife to carve a smiley – or scary if you prefer – face. Pop a tealight inside for the full effect.

Waste not Don't waste the flesh of your pumpkin. It's traditional to use it to make soup or pumpkin pie.

Squashes

Squashes are divided up into two categories: winter and summer types. Summer squashes come in a wide range of sizes and colours, and are very closely related to courgettes and marrows. Winter squashes are tougher, beefier vegetables, akin to pumpkins, but with a nuttier, sweeter taste and a wide range of quirky and unusual shapes. Both are easy to grow.

Planting out Seedlings can be planted out once the risk of frosts is over but will need watering daily until they get established.

Storing & Using

They can be used in: soups ...stews...stir-fries...or roasted...or baked...

Winter squashes can be stored for up to 6 months in a cool, dry place. "Cure" them first by hardening the skin in a sunny spot, but keep them dry. The skin of summer squashes doesn't harden as much as winter squashes, so these can't be kept as long.

Roasted Peeled, sliced, drizzled with olive oil and sprinkled with fresh, aromatic herbs, squashes can be oven-roasted to make a tasty side dish.

Growing

If you want a bumper crop from your squashes, you must give them a rich, fertile soil in full sun. If you are restricted for space, try growing some of the smaller-fruiting varieties up vertical supports such as pergolas, trellises and posts.

◆ **SOW SEEDS UNDER COVER** from mid- to late spring, individually in 7.5cm (3in) pots and 1cm (½in) deep. Sow them on their sides to prevent them rotting. Leave them to germinate on a sunny window ledge, then plant them out 1.5m (5ft) apart when there is no further risk of spring frosts.

◆ **ALTERNATIVELY**, sow directly outdoors after the risk of frost is over, sowing two or three seeds 2.5cm (1in) deep and 1.5m (5ft) apart. Thin the seedlings out to leave the strongest and cover with fleece or a cloche if a late frost is forecast.

'Queensland Blue'

'Sweet Dumpling'

butternut

Squash bed

If you have poor, infertile soil on your allotment, do not despair. You can easily and cheaply construct a squash bed, where you can provide the perfect growing conditions for your beautiful crop. The bed can be as big as you have room for. The cardboard base retains moisture and nutrients, and eventually rots away. Feed the squashes regularly to ensure a large crop.

Cardboard base Lay pieces of cardboard on the bare soil and create a retaining wall all around from brick and stones or timber.

Organic matter Add plenty of organic matter to the bed, such as well-rotted manure or good garden compost.

Plant and water Space the plants at least 1.2m (4ft) apart and water them every few days throughout the summer.

Routine care

Because they produce so much luxuriant foliage and their fruit has such a high water content, squashes are really thirsty plants, so make sure you visit the plot regularly throughout the summer to give them plenty of water.

◆ **SUPPORT SQUASHES** on a piece of wood, tile or straw to stop them rotting on the ground as they start to swell. Regularly tie in the growth if you are training them up posts and stakes.

◆ **TOUGHEN UP** squashes for storing over winter, by leaving the fruit to mature on the plant for as long as possible before the first frosts arrive. Don't allow frost to get to the fruit or it will turn mushy and won't keep for long.

Netting Some squashes have a trailing habit and, if space is limited, can be trained vertically. As the fruits start to swell, they will need support. Here, a fruit net from shop-bought fruit does the job.

'Turk's Turban'

'Little Gem'

patty pan

Peppers & Chillies

Coming in a range of vibrant colours, peppers and chillies spice up your allotment with eye-catching fruits, as well as enhancing your cooking. Peppers put the crunch into salads while chillies vary from mild to fiery hot. Match your culinary preference to your plant choice.

Sowing

Sow seeds indoors in early spring, placing the pots in a heated propagator until the seedlings have sprouted.

Pots Place seeds 1cm (½in) deep in seed compost in individual pots and water well. Once the seedlings have emerged, move to a warm window ledge.

Planting out When all danger of frost has passed, space plants at 40cm (16in) apart in the soil. Water thoroughly after planting.

Growing

Peppers and chillies are suitable for growing outdoors on the allotment if there is a warm, sunny site available. Alternatively, they can be grown in the greenhouse but this means having to get down to the allotment each day to water the plants. If the allotment is in a frost pocket, then you should definitely grow them under cover.

◆ **CHILLIES AND PEPPERS** can either be grown in the ground or in frost-resistant containers that are at least 25cm (10in) wide. Plants can also be planted into growbags but these will need watering every day.

◆ **IF PLANTING OUTDOORS**, the seedlings should be hardened off for a few days, either by putting them in a cold frame or by placing them outdoors during the day and bringing them back in at night.

◆ **PINCH OUT** the growing tips when the plants are about 25cm (10in) high to encourage the plants to grow more bushy. This should produce more fruits. Once you see flowers on the plants, start giving them a weekly liquid feed to help them develop and then produce fruit.

Water Keep plants well watered throughout the summer to produce a good crop. Dry spells can result in fewer fruits on the plants.

habanero   'Cascabel'   'Aji Limon'   'Aji'   'Ring of Fire' purple pepper   red pepper   yellow pepper

Support

As they grow, the plants will need supporting with canes and soft garden twine to prevent the stems snapping.

Root care When inserting the cane into the soil, take care not to damage the roots of the plants.

Routine care

If you are growing plants in the greenhouse, flying insects won't be able to reach the flowers to pollinate them so they will need assistance. Stroke the insides of the flowers with a small paintbrush to pass the pollen from one flower to another.

◆ **HARVEST** the fruits when they are green or when they have fully coloured up. Use secateurs to remove them from the plant.

◆ **PLACE A CLOCHE** over the pepper plants to protect them if they haven't ripened before autumn.

Storing & Using

They can be used for: con carne...chilli oil...or dried...or roasted...or frozen...or bottled...

Peppers go mushy when frozen, but can be used in soups and stews. Chillies are best stored dried, but can also be frozen and will keep for up to a year in the freezer. Dry in the sun on a wire mesh, or hang up in the kitchen. Always wash your hands after handling chillies.

Chilli oil Chillies can be used to infuse cooking oil or can be diced and added to relishes.

Drying Thread chillies onto lengths of string then hang them up to dry in the kitchen.

pimento   'Hungarian Hot Wax'   'Poblano'   Scotch bonnet   cayenne

Sweetcorn

Tall, leafy and upright, sweetcorn is one of the most attractive crops to grow on the allotment. It is also one of the most worthwhile, as the cobs quickly lose their sweetness once picked, which you will only appreciate fully when you cook your own, straight from the plants. The cobs can be boiled, grilled or cooked directly on the barbecue.

Ready When the tassels of the sweetcorn begin to turn brown, check if the cobs are ready to eat (see right).

Growing

Growing tubes If you sow the seeds in cardboard tubes, you can plant out the entire tube to avoid disturbing the roots of the plants.

To give your crop a head start, sow seed under cover in late spring. Fill small pots or module trays with seed compost, water lightly, then sow one seed in each pot or module. Seed can also be sown directly outside (see below).

♦ **THE SEED** should be planted 2cm (¾in) deep and then covered over with compost. Place in a heated propagator or on a warm sunny windowsill.

♦ **SEEDLINGS CAN** be planted out after the risk of spring frosts has passed. The plants should be about 10cm (4in) tall before planting out.

♦ **SWEETCORN** relies on being pollinated by the wind, which is most successful if they are planted in a grid pattern, where the pollen can blow from plant to plant. Position plants 30 x 30cm (12 x 12in) apart.

Sowing outdoors

It is possible to sow seeds directly into the soil from mid-spring onward, which is useful if you don't have a greenhouse. Warm the soil using a cloche for about two weeks before sowing. Make small planting holes, 2cm (¾in) deep, spaced 30cm (12in) apart in a grid pattern, and sow two seeds in each. Cover the seeds with soil. Replace the cloche until the seeds germinate, then thin the seedlings to leave the strongest per pair.

Sowing Sow two seeds in each hole to double your chances of successful germination. Not all seeds will come up or survive.

Germination When the seedlings start to emerge, they should be thinned out to the strongest plant.

Protecting plants Recycle your plastic bottles or milk cartons to use as extra weather protection for the plants.

Growing tips

Sweetcorn varieties should not be allowed to cross pollinate each other because this can spoil the cobs. Either grow one variety or plant different varieties well apart from each other. As the plants get taller, they will need staking with canes to provide support. To make best use of the space, grow low-growing squashes beneath sweetcorn plants, which trail across the soil.

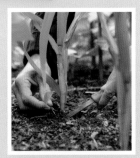

Weeding Weed regularly around the base of the plants to prevent any weeds from competing for nutrients.

Mounding As the plants develop, mound the soil up around their bases to provide additional support to the tall stems.

Watering Plants will need watering every few days, particularly after planting and at flowering time.

Harvesting

Sweetcorn is harvested by firmly twisting the cobs from the plant. You can expect two or three cobs from a healthy plant.
◆ **TO TEST** if they're ready, peel back the outer leaves and press your thumb nail into a kernel. If a milky sap runs out of it, they're ready for harvesting. If not, wrap the leaves back around the cob and check it a few days later.

When to harvest
Sweetcorn cobs soon lose their sweetness once ripe. Check them regularly and harvest them as soon as possible.

Storing & Using

It can be used for: soups...corn bread...relish...or can be roasted...or frozen...

Ideally, eat the sweetcorn as soon as possible after harvesting to enjoy the natural sweetness and flavour to its full. Harvested cobs can be kept in a fridge for no longer than a day or two at the most. Frozen cobs keep well for around 6 months.

Freezing Like peas, cobs can often taste sweeter after freezing. Freeze whole or, if space is limited, remove kernels and then freeze.

Relish
Sweetcorn kernels can be added to relishes and chutneys, providing natural sweetness and colour.

Corn bread
Savoury corn bread is a tasty and traditional dish. It can be flavoured using chillies, cheese or herbs.

sweetcorn

Globe artichokes

Adding a wonderful ornamental element to the allotment plot with their architectural, silvery foliage and stunning bright purple flower heads, globe artichokes are also a gourmet feast. They are large plants but don't expect heavy crops – the edible flower hearts are a harvest of quality not quantity.

Hardening off Harden off seedlings for a few days in a porch or cold frame before planting out.

Seeds and offsets

Artichokes can be grown from seed in mid-spring but should not be allowed to crop in their first year, and will yield only sparingly their second. Mature plants crop more freely.

Sowing Lightly water the compost before sowing the seeds thinly in trays at a depth of 2cm (¾in). Grow the plants on until large enough to plant outside.

New plants Artichokes can be grown from leafy buds, or "offsets", that form at the base of the parent plant. Cut them off in spring, pot up, and grow them on.

Growing

These are a real luxury crop to grow as they take up lots of space in relation to their yield. However, they are well worth the effort, as they taste amazing and are expensive to buy. The plants require a sheltered position in full sun, in rich but well-drained soil.

◆ **DUE TO** their elegant and stately habit, you might want to consider planting artichokes among the flower border, rather than the vegetable patch on the allotment.

◆ **BEAR IN MIND** when deciding where to grow artichokes that they are large perennial plants and require plenty of space over a prolonged period. They are, therefore, not ideal for smaller plots.

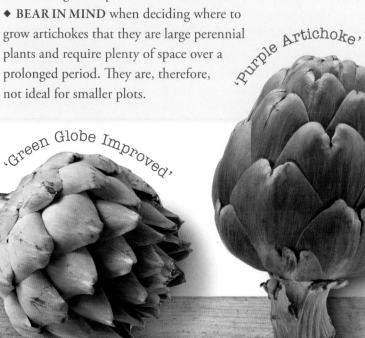

'Green Globe Improved'

'Purple Artichoke'

Flowers Allotment holders have to choose between whether to harvest the artichokes or allow the striking purple, thistle-like flowers to develop each year.

Overwintering

Artichokes are perennial and are at their most productive for about three or four years after planting. When the plants start to die back in autumn the dead material should be removed to prevent any build-up of disease.

Cutting back After harvesting, the plants should be cut back and a thick layer of mulch added to suppress weeds and protect the central growing point.

Routine care

Seedlings and offsets should be planted out in late spring, spacing the plants 90cm (3ft) apart. Remove any flower buds that appear in the first year to encourage strong growth.

◆ **KEEP THE SOIL** around the plants well mulched with garden compost and water regularly during dry periods, particularly while the plants are young.

◆ **HARVEST BY** removing the artichoke head using secateurs when it is about the size of a golf ball. If left too long, the flower will start to open, and the hearts will become inedible.

Ready to eat Cut the artichoke buds when they reach full size but before the outer scales have begun to open.

Storing & Using

They can be: steamed...boiled... chargrilled...added to salads or risottos...

Cut and cook artichokes straight away, or store in the fridge for a day or two at most. Don't freeze them. They are delicious with garlic mayonnaise, or lemon and olive oil dressings.

Division Plants can be divided after three or four years – use two forks back-to-back to do this. Offshoots can be potted on as replacement plants.

vegetables

beans & pods

French & runner beans
- a runner bean support
- broad beans
- peas & mangetout

French & Runner beans

Brightly coloured flowers scrambling up a rustic wigwam structure is a classic image on an allotment site. Runner beans are more rampant than French beans but both require structures to climb up, providing not only a splash of colour on the plot, but also height to what could otherwise be a flat-looking veggie patch.

'Purple Teepee'

Sowing

Both types of beans can be sown indoors or outside in late spring. Sowing under cover gets them off to a faster start, but outdoors is fine, and means you don't have to harden them off before planting out.

Indoors Fill small plastic pots or cardboard growing tubes with multi-purpose compost. Make a 5cm (2in) deep hole, sow the seed and fill the hole.

Outdoors Make a 5cm (2in) deep hole directly into the soil. Place two seeds in each hole. After the seeds have germinated, remove the weaker plant of the two.

Growing

If you have sown your seeds indoors they will need planting out in early summer, once the risk of frost has passed. Choose a sheltered location in full sun. Thoroughly dig over the area to be planted, remove any weeds from the site, and add plenty of organic material, such as well-rotted manure or garden compost.

◆ **WATER REGULARLY** throughout the summer, especially once the plants start to flower and produce pods. Dry spells can cause the flowers to die back and developing pods may wither.

◆ **THE BEANS** are ready for harvesting when they reach about 15cm (6in) long. Pick runner beans before the pods start to swell, or they will lose their tenderness and become tough and stringy.

◆ **KEEP PICKING** regularly, almost every day, to keep the plants in full production. Otherwise they will quickly turn to seed and stop cropping. French beans can be harvested for their pods or as mature beans, depending on variety.

French beans

Support

Climbing beans require supports, which are commonly made from tall sticks or bamboo canes, at least 2.1–2.4m (7–8ft) tall. These can be arranged as circular wigwams, or as double rows joined across the top to form a long, rigid structure. The uprights should be placed 20–23cm (8–9in) apart.

◆ **AS PLANTS GROW** they may need tying to their supports at first. After this they will naturally climb up the structures using their twining stems to grip the uprights. Particularly vigorous plants may occasionally need tying in throughout the season. Pinch out the growing tips when they reach the top to encourage plants to produce new stems and more beans.

◆ **IT IS BEST** to have the supports in place first before planting, to avoid damaging the plants later.

Support structure Bamboo canes and tall sticks both make very good supports for beans. Position one plant at the base of each support.

Growing tips

Both types of beans are relatively trouble free. Runner bean leaves can be prone to wind damage, leaving them tattered. Keep damaged plants well watered to aid recovery.

Protection Upside down plastic bottles protect young plants from slug attack and from late-spring frosts.

Tying in Occasional wayward shoots may need tying into the climbing structure as the beans grow.

Mulching Beans will benefit from a layer of mulch around their roots to help retain soil moisture.

Storing & Using

They can be used for: relish...chutney...casseroles... salads...or can be frozen...

French and runner beans are best eaten fresh, but can be stored in the fridge for a few days. French beans can be left to develop fully in their pods, which when dried can be used as haricots. Store them in an airtight container for up to a year, and use them in casseroles and bean salads. Both runner and French beans can be frozen; blanch first, then dry well, and freeze. They will keep well in the freezer for up to 9 months.

Chutney Runner beans often produce a glut. There are lots of exciting bean chutney recipes that will allow you to enjoy your harvest all year.

runner beans

Project
Runner bean support

Runner beans are very easy to grow and can be started off in pots under glass in early May. By June they will be ready to plant out but, being climbing plants, they will need a good support system. This project features the traditional and very common double-row method that makes care of your crop and harvesting far easier.

The canes should be inserted at an angle sloping towards the middle of the plot so that each pair of canes almost touches at the top.

step 2

Alternative shapes

Being such active climbers, runner beans will happily find their way up any nearby structure. If you don't have room for the traditional double row of canes shown here, then trellis or garden fencing with vertical wires attached to it will work just as well. You could also make an attractive arch using flexible hazel canes.

The soil should be prepared before planting. Dig it over thoroughly and add plenty of organic material. Well-rotted compost or leaf mould are ideal choices. These will help the soil to retain moisture.

step 1

Popular pyramids A pyramid is a popular shape for supporting runner beans. Insert four canes in the ground at the corners of an imaginary square and tie the tops of the four canes together.

MATERIALS & TOOLS

• bamboo or hazel canes, 2.4m (8ft) long (the quantity required will depend on the length of your plot), garden twine

1 Push in the first of your canes at one corner of the plot. Using another cane as a guide for a straight line, continue pushing the canes in at intervals of 15–30cm (6–12in).

2 Once the row is complete, repeat the procedure with the other set of canes, positioning them 45–60cm (18–24in) away and parallel to the first row.

step 3

step 4

The top and final cane anchors the pairs of canes securely and helps to keep them properly spaced as the runner beans grow.

Tie the twine around the canes tightly so that the completed structure is rigid and there is no risk of it collapsing.

Plants can be encouraged to grow upwards by gently wrapping their stems around the canes. You can use a little loosely wound twine to hold the stems in place until they get going.

step 5

Ensure you have easy access to both sides of your runner bean supports so you can easily pinch out the tips of plants that have reached the top, and to make it easy to harvest your crop.

3   With all the canes in place, lay another cane horizontally across the top so that it sits in the natural cradle created by the other canes.

4   Securely tie the horizontal cane to each pair of canes, starting at one end and working your way across to the other end.

5   Plant a runner-bean plant in a prepared hole at the base of each cane. Fill the hole with soil, then gently firm it in place.

Broad beans

Broad beans are one of the first vegetables to harvest down on the allotment and many plotters compete to see who will be the first to pick their fresh crop of these small and succulent vegetables each spring. Their sweetly scented white flowers are also fantastic for attracting bees and many other pollinating insects.

Watering Keep young plants well watered; they will soon develop a deep tap root to reach groundwater supplies.

Sowing outdoors In dry weather, water the drill first, then sow the bean seeds, cover over and firm the soil.

Sowing outdoors

In milder areas it is possible to sow broad beans directly outdoors in autumn for an early crop the following spring. To do this it is necessary to use hardy varieties such as 'Aquadulce' and 'The Sutton'. Otherwise they should be sown outdoors in early or mid spring.

◆ **PRIOR TO** sowing prepare the soil well by digging it over and raking it level. Broad beans are more tolerant of poor soils than other beans.

◆ **SOW BEANS** 5cm (2in) deep and 20cm (8in) apart, although there are dwarf varieties that can be sown at closer distances.

Sowing under cover

If you are on an exposed allotment site or in a cold region, making autumn outdoor sowing unrealistic, then seeds can be sown under cover in mid- to late winter. Seeds should be sown 5cm (2in) deep in general-purpose compost and kept watered during germination.

Pots Use growing tubes or cardboard toilet roll tubes to help the long tap roots get established.

Harden off Harden off the plants in a cold frame or at home in the porch before planting out.

Plant out Plant them 20cm (8in) apart and be prepared to cover with fleece in cold weather.

Routine care

Plants that have been started indoors may get frost-damaged, so be ready with some fleece if cold weather is forecast. Taller varieties will need support, so push twiggy branches in amongst emerging plants. Give the soil a thorough soaking during dry periods in the spring, particularly during flowering. Make successional sowings (that is, sow a new batch every three weeks or so) through early and mid-spring to extend the growing season into summer.

◆ **BEANS SHOULD** be ready about 10 weeks after sowing in spring. Pick the pods when they are young, starting at the base of the plant and working upwards as the season progresses.

◆ **WHEN THE PLANTS** have finished producing pods, cut them down to ground level. This allows the roots to break down in the soil and provide a free supply of nitrogen for the next crop.

Growing tips

Pinching back the growing tip encourages an even earlier spring crop. Pinching out the tip also reduces damage by the black bean aphid, which attacks the young shoots.

Pinching back Pinch back the growing tip by about 7.5cm (3in) when the first pods start to form along the stem. The tips can be eaten.

Companion planting Growing the poached egg plant near broad beans attracts hoverflies, which feed on blackfly.

Storing & Using

They can be used for: risotto...soups...stews...dips...or frozen...

Broad beans are incredibly versatile and deliciously tender when young and fresh. They can be kept in the fridge for a few days or can be frozen for up to 6 months. Use older beans for soups and stews. Cook fresh young beans until al dente, combined with a little garlic, butter and herbs to make a side dish with meat or fish.

Double skinning Once podded, you can slit the skin of the bean with your nail and peel off the outer skin for extra tenderness.

Dip Make a delicious dip by blending young cooked beans with crème fraîche, dill and lemon juice.

broad beans

Peas & Mangetout

These climbing and scrambling plants are an allotment must; there is nothing quite like their sweet taste and crunchy texture when picked fresh and they are costly to buy in the shops. If space is a problem, then consider growing some of the dwarf varieties.

Healthy snack Mangetout are a children's favourite and must be one of the most healthy raw takeaway snacks available. Keep picking to ensure they keep producing delicious pods.

Sowing indoors

Sow peas and mangetout indoors in February or March, or outside in spring. Alternatively, sow them indoors in autumn for an early crop the following season.

Sow in pots Place a couple of seeds into small plastic pots filled with good-quality compost. Seeds should be about 5cm (2in) deep.

Thin out Keep the plants warm and well watered. Thin out the weaker shoots and plant the stronger ones out in spring when all danger of frost is over.

Growing

Peas and mangetout require a position in full sun that is sheltered from strong winds to prevent pollinating insects from being blown away when they visit their flowers. Peas require lots of moisture in the soil so they can produce masses of flowers and pods during the summer.

◆ **TO HOLD MOISTURE** in the soil, dig out a trench 30cm (12in) deep in autumn and fill it with well-rotted compost, kitchen waste and shredded newspaper.

◆ **COVER IT** over with a 5cm (2in) layer of soil and leave it to rot down for a few weeks prior to sowing or planting.

Sowing outside

Peas either have smooth or wrinkly skins. The smooth-skinned ones are hardier and more suitable for early sowings, while the wrinkly skinned types produce sweeter crops. Sow every three or four weeks until midsummer for a long season.

Sowing Sow seeds in trenches 5cm (2in) deep, 12cm (5in) wide and 8cm (3in) apart.

Thin out Keep seedlings well watered and thin out any that are growing too close together.

Routine care

Apart from providing support (see right) and plenty of water (see below), peas and mangetout don't have many special requirements.

◆ **PLANTS NEED** to be kept well watered, particularly during the flowering period and when they are producing their pods. Healthy, well-watered plants are also less prone to mildew.

◆ **WATCH OUT FOR BIRDS**, particularly pigeons, which love stripping off the pea shoots. Covering the plants with a net will help to protect them.

◆ **KEEP PICKING** peas and mangetout as they mature and sow regularly to be able to harvest throughout the summer.

Support

Unless you are growing dwarf varieties, peas and mangetout need support to scramble up. Choose from pea sticks, netting or chicken wire.

Sticks Peas sticks are the most effective method of support. Insert twiggy branches next to the plants when they are 7.5cm (3in) high.

Training Keep a watch out for any wayward stems and hook them back onto the twigs, should any be growing away from their support.

Storing & Using

They can be used for: soups...stir-fries...salads...or can be frozen...

Both peas and mangetout keep in the fridge for a few days. Mangetout are flat-podded peas eaten whole, hence the French name, which means "eat everything". Crisp and sweet, they can be eaten raw in salads, boiled, steamed or used in stir-fries.

Soup Fresh peas make a delicious soup with some mint and a swirl of cream or some crème fraîche.

Frozen Peas are one of the few vegetables that almost benefit from freezing. Picked and frozen immediately, they retain their sweetness and can be kept in the freezer for up to 9 months.

peas in their pods

mangetout

vegetables

bulbs & roots

potatoes • carrots • sweet potatoes • onions & shallots • garlic • spring onions • a drying rack • florence fennel & kohl rabi • celeriac & parsnips • swedes & turnips • beetroot • radishes • jerusalem artichokes

Potatoes

There are three types of potatoes, named after the period when they are ready – hence earlies, second earlies, and maincrop. It is definitely worth growing these on the allotment, but if you are short of space, avoid maincrop varieties, which are bulky. Instead, focus on growing new potatoes and salad types, which also have the best flavour.

Chitting

Get your potatoes off to an early start by getting them to sprout, or "chit", before planting. This method is particularly useful on cold, wet soil for early or new potatoes.

Early start Place seed potatoes with their rose ends (where the buds are) facing upwards in egg boxes in a light, cool, frost-free place until they sprout.

Growing

Plant early and second early potatoes in early spring; maincrops can be planted in mid-spring. To plant, dig a trench 20cm (8in) deep and place the seed potatoes along the bottom at spacings of 45cm (18in) for early potatoes, 70cm (28in) for maincrops.

◆ **MAKE SURE** the potatoes are the right way up with their eyes, or "chits", facing upwards. Mix well-rotted manure or compost with the soil from the trench, and use to cover over the potatoes.

◆ **POTATOES** require a sunny site, ideally with heavy, rich soil. If you have an overgrown allotment, planting potatoes will help to break up the soil.

◆ **ONLY PLANT** seed potatoes that are certified virus-free, and don't raise plants from tubers left in the soil from last year, which can harbour disease.

Planting in bags If you are short of space, grow potatoes in large bags or special potato bags. Tip the plants out to harvest the tubers or carefully dig them up.

Planting When the sprouts are about 2.5cm (1in) long, the potatoes are ready to be planted out into holes or trenches.

'Arran Victory' 'Dunbar Rover' 'Estima' 'Jersey Royal'

Protection Early-emerging shoots can be susceptible to frost damage, so make sure they are covered with garden fleece.

Earthing up

As the shoots emerge they need earthing up – covering the base of plants with soil. This helps to prevent frost damage, stops the growing tubers from turning green, and encourages a larger crop.

Cover up To earth up potatoes, use a spade or rake to push soil up around the base of the shoots, ensuring the soil doesn't cover the foliage.

Routine care

Once planted, potatoes need little routine care and are among the easiest crops to grow. Young plants should be weeded regularly to prevent competition for moisture and nutrients. Mature plants form canopies of leaves that suppress most weeds.

◆ **KEEP THE PLANTS** well watered as they grow, especially during dry spells. If kept too dry, the plants will produce smaller tubers and poorer harvests.

◆ **FEED THE PLANTS** regularly using a balanced, granular fertilizer.

◆ **CHECK THE TUBERS** by scraping back the soil carefully, to see if they are ready to harvest – re-cover if not.

◆ **FOR AN EARLY START**, try growing potatoes in rubber tyres, which will insulate them from spring frosts.

Harvest Potatoes are ready for harvesting just after flowering. Use a garden fork to dig up the potatoes, being careful not to damage the tubers.

Storing & Using

They can be: mashed…boiled…fried…roasted… baked…chipped…au gratin…

Potatoes are probably the most popular and versatile of vegetables. New potatoes, such as 'Wilja' or 'Nicola', are great in salads. Use maincrops, such as 'Rooster', for mash, 'King Edward' for baking and chipping, and 'Arran Victory' for roasting.

Storing Thick paper sacks are ideal for storage. Kept in a cool, dark place, the potatoes will store well for 2–3 months or more.

'King Edward' 'Wilja' 'Nicola' 'Vivaldi' 'Rooster'

Carrots

These delicious, sweet and crunchy roots are a real favourite with children, and if stored correctly, they can be enjoyed all year round. Consider growing them in raised beds if you have stony or heavy soil. For something different consider growing the purple varieties, the original colour of carrots prior to the 17th century.

Sowing

Avoid using old seeds and check the expiry dates on packets, as this can often be the cause of poor or no germination. Carrots should be directly sown into the soil in spring.

Starting off Make a drill, 2cm (¾in) deep, and sow seeds lightly. Use fleece early in the year to protect against frost.

Thinning out When they emerge, thin out the seedlings. Check the seed packet for their space requirements.

Growing carrots

There are a wide range of carrot varieties to grow, but they all generally prefer light, well-drained soil in full sun. If the soil on the allotment is heavy or stony, then consider growing them in raised beds. Alternatively, try growing the short or round varieties such as 'Parmex', which cope better in these conditions.

◆ **DIG OVER** the beds thoroughly before sowing, removing any large stones and weeds. Improve the soil with well-rotted organic matter. Avoid using fresh manure, which causes roots to split.

◆ **IN SPRING** sow seeds in batches, every 2–3 weeks, to give a prolonged harvest. The seeds can be slow to germinate so don't give up too soon.

Watering Keep young seedlings well watered in dry spells to assist the plants to develop, and their roots to swell.

heritage carrots

Carrot fly This pest can quickly destroy a crop. Prevent damage by erecting a 60cm (24in) barrier of insect mesh around the crop to prevent the low-flying adults landing.

short, round carrots

long, stump-rooted carrots

Routine care

If growing carrots early on in the year, they will need covering with fleece to speed up germination and to protect the seedlings. Lift the fleece on warmer days to maximize the light reaching the plants.

Keep the plants well watered in dry spells and regularly weed around them, being careful not to damage their roots.

◆ **CARROT FLY** (see p.232) is the main pest to look out for; its larvae will tunnel into the roots and ruin the crop. Thinning, harvesting and even weeding can release the carrots' scent, attracting the pest, so do these jobs in the evening when the insects are inactive.

◆ **IF THERE IS** a major problem with carrot fly on the allotment, consider using resistant varieties such as 'Flyaway'.

Harvesting Lift carrots once they reach the desired size. Early varieties should be pulled when young, tender and juicy.

Storing & Using

They can be used for: soups...stews...stir-fries... or boiled...or roasted...

Carrots will keep for a few days in the fridge, or blanch them and store in the freezer for up to 9 months.

In sand Carrots last for weeks stored in boxes of slightly damp sand, kept in a cool, dark place.

long, pointed carrots

Sweet potatoes

Sweet potatoes are a wonderful alternative to the humble spud. Traditionally considered an exotic crop from warm climates, recently developed varieties enable allotment holders living in cooler parts of the world to enjoy this delicious vegetable, too. Low in fat and packed full of vitamins and antioxidants, sweet potatoes are definitely worth giving a go.

Watering This crop needs regular watering – daily in dry weather. To avoid visiting the allotment so often, cut plastic bottles in half, push them into the soil alongside the plants and fill with water.

Growing

Sweet potatoes require a temperature of at least 21°C (70°F) to produce their tasty underground tubers. In cooler climates, you will need to grow them in a polytunnel, cloche or greenhouse. In warmer areas they can be grown outdoors, but will benefit from being planted in a hole cut through black, weed-suppressing membrane to help maintain the temperature of the soil.

◆ **MAIL-ORDER PLANTS** arrive in spring as "slips", or rooted cuttings. As soon as they arrive, plunge the slips into a bucket of water indoors to revitalize them, then pot them on into individual pots in general-purpose compost the following day. Keep the slips indoors for three weeks before planting them out.

◆ **SWEET POTATOES** are space-hungry, eventually becoming large, vigorous, sprawling plants, so make sure you have enough room for them. They should be planted 30cm (12in) apart in rows 75cm (30in) apart.

◆ **THEY REQUIRE** a sheltered, fertile, warm site in well-drained soil. Dig the soil over thoroughly prior to planting and add plenty of well-rotted organic matter.

Pruning

Sweet potatoes are vigorous, sprawling plants whose growth must be kept in check if they are to focus their energy on producing a crop – and to prevent them smothering other plants. If you are growing them in a greenhouse, you can train the stems onto a support system to keep them out of the way. When cutting back new growth (see right), save the leaves and cook as you would spinach.

Encouraging laterals Regularly prune back the new growth to encourage more laterals to develop on the plant.

sweet potato

Storing & Using

They can be used in: soups...curries...risottos...
mash...chips...or roasted...or sautéed...or frozen...

Sweet potatoes are neither very sweet nor very moist
when they are first harvested, so keep them in a
warm place for a week to "cure" them before eating.
If preferred, after curing, move them to a cool, dark
place and you can keep them for about a month. If
you want to freeze your crop, cook
them first. They will keep for up
to 12 months in the freezer.

Tortilla Teamed with spring onions
and red chilli, this tortilla makes a
tasty light lunch or elegant supper
dish served with a fresh, green salad.

Bake Sweet
potatoes can
be oven-baked
like an ordinary
potato and filled
with a range of
toppings.

Sweet chips Tossed in oil and
soy sauce or dried chilli flakes,
these sweet potato chips make a
good accompaniment to home-made
burgers or chicken dishes
and contain more fibre
than traditional potatoes.
Serve with soured cream.

Routine care

Feed the sweet potato plants with a good, general-purpose
fertilizer every few weeks.

◆ **WATER EVERY FEW DAYS** in dry weather (see
opposite) and particularly if you are growing them
under cover. Keep the greenhouse, polytunnel or
cloche well ventilated on warm days.

◆ **THE FOLIAGE** turning brown and starting to die,
about three months after planting, is a sign that they
are ready to harvest. Dig them up, making sure that
you don't spike them with the fork, or leave them in
the ground for longer if preferred, but make sure to
lift them before the first autumnal frosts.

Harvesting Sweet
potato tubers grow
underground like
common or garden
potatoes and are
harvested in the
same way. They
come in a huge
range of colours,
including orange
and purple, which
add a splash of
colour to the plate.

'Boniato'

Onions & Shallots

The humble onion has to be the number one essential vegetable to grow on the allotment if you enjoy cooking, as they appear in most culinary dishes. Shallots are a smaller, more delicately flavoured version but they still pack a punch in terms of taste and versatility in the kitchen.

Sowing indoors

Onion seeds can be sown under cover from midwinter to mid-spring. Sowing onions from seeds takes longer than planting sets, but is cheaper to do, and there is a wider range of varieties to choose.

Sowing seeds Fill module trays or small plastic pots with good-quality seed compost and sow clusters of seeds in each one, 1cm (½in) deep.

Thinning seedlings When the seedlings are about 7.5cm (3in) tall they should be thinned out to leave the strongest one in each pot or module.

Growing

Onions and shallots are one of the easiest and least demanding crops to grow. Onion seeds can either be sown indoors (see left) or directly in the soil. However, they are more commonly grown from "sets" (see below). The plants require a sheltered location in well-drained soil in full sun. They prefer light soils, as they can be prone to rotting in heavy, wet conditions.

- ◆ **TRY GROWING** them in raised beds if the soil is unsuitable.
- ◆ **SHALLOTS GROW** very slowly from seed, so it is recommended that they are planted as sets in early spring or autumn, at 15cm (6in) intervals, in rows 30cm (12in) apart.

Grow bunches Instead of thinning the seedlings, onions and shallots can be left to grow in bunches, giving a large number of smaller bulbs.

Planting sets

The easiest method of growing onions is to plant "sets". These are baby bulbs that grow on and mature once planted. Planting time is usually spring, although overwintering-types and Japanese onions can also be planted in autumn.

Spacing Onions sets should be spaced at 5–10cm (2–4in) intervals, in rows that are 30cm (12in) apart.

Firming in Push the sets firmly into the soil leaving just the tips poking out above the surface.

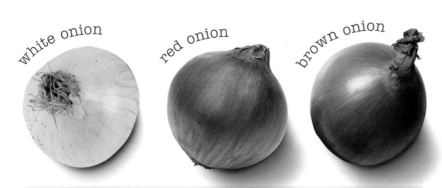

white onion   red onion   brown onion

Onions and shallots are ready to lift when the foliage yellows and dies back. Bend the leaves over as the bulbs mature.

Onions Mature bulbs should have dry, crisp outer skins before they are harvested and stored. Leave them to dry.

Shallots Mature shallots form clusters of small bulbs, which are split and used individually in the kitchen.

Routine care

Onions and shallots are relatively trouble free. Keep them well watered during dry periods but be careful not to overwater them, as onions will start to rot if they sit in wet soil for too long. Stop watering completely as the bulbs start to mature, as the excess moisture will prevent the bulbs from drying after harvesting.

◆ **CAREFULLY WEED** between plants to prevent competition for nutrients. A short-handled onion hoe is useful to reach weeds in the gaps without damaging the bulbs.

◆ **ONIONS THAT** were planted or sown in autumn should be ready for harvesting in midsummer, whereas spring-raised plants will be ready in summer and autumn.

◆ **ONIONS AND SHALLOTS** should be dried in the sun before taking them indoors for storage. If the weather is dry, leave them on the soil surface for a day or two.

Storing & Using

They can be used in: sauces…stews…casseroles…onion tart…French onion soup… or can be pickled…or strung…

Onions and shallots store very well if dried properly and can keep for up to a year hanging up in the kitchen. Red onions are good for slicing into salads, while brown ones are stronger and are better cooked. Shallots are ideal for risottos and also delicious caramelized as a side dish.

Pickled Onions pickled in vinegar and spices will keep in the cupboard for a year.

Strung up Onions can be plaited by their dry stalks and hung up for storage; cut off and use as needed.

'Longor'   'Biztro'   'Jermor'   'Delvad'

Garlic

Make sure you leave space for this essential allotment crop.
Renowned as being one of the most pungent and aromatic of all
the vegetables, garlic has a wonderful flavour and aroma. It is a
key ingredient in cooking and is said to be beneficial to health.

Flowers Cut off most garlic
flowers you see forming, leaving
a few for dried flower displays.

Buying bulbs

Always buy certified virus-free
stock from reputable suppliers
and choose varieties suitable to
your growing conditions. Don't
simply buy supermarket bulbs,
as they are imported and are
unsuitable for our climate.

Healthy cloves Discard any spindly,
withered, or under-sized cloves as they
won't grow into large bulbs.

Growing

Garlic requires a warm, sheltered and
sunny site with well-drained soil. It is
a useful crop to grow, as it is planted in
autumn and grows through the winter,
when the beds are otherwise empty. Garlic can also be planted
in spring, although the bulbs produced will be smaller.

◆ **PLANT GARLIC** by breaking open the bulbs and pushing
the individual cloves into the soil or in pots, leaving just their
tip poking out above the surface of the soil or compost.

◆ **THEY CAN** also be started under cover in small pots to speed
up their development, before planting out once they have
produced strong growth. Cloves should be planted 15cm (6in)
apart. Keep the area well-watered and free of competing weeds.

◆ **THE CLOVES** should swell into generous-sized bulbs with the
autumn-planted ones ready to harvest in early summer; spring-
planted bulbs mature from midsummer onwards.

Storing & Using

Garlic can be used in: sauces...stews...
risottos...or can be slow-roasted...

Garlic stores well for up to nine months
when dried and hung in a cool, dry place.
It is invaluable for sauces with onions
and tomatoes, and adds a tang to
potato wedges. Try making garlic
sauce using bread crumbs or
potatoes, olive oil, and lemon
juice, to serve with fish or
chicken dishes.

garlic bulb

Spring onions

This is a quick and easy crop to grow that takes up little space, and can even be raised in patio containers. Spring onions add a fresh, mild-onion flavour to summer salads and Asian cooking, and there are many varieties to try.

Growing

Spring onions prefer fertile, well-drained soil in full sun. They are raised from seed, usually outdoors, but can be started under cover, before planting them outside three weeks later, for an earlier crop.

◆ **SOW OUTDOORS** directly into shallow drills that are 2cm (¾in) deep, in rows 30cm (12in) apart, leaving about 1cm (½in) between each plant. Spring onions are very fast growing – during summer they can be ready within about five weeks after sowing.

◆ **SPRING ONIONS** are ready for harvesting when the stems are about 1–2cm (½–¾in) thick, and about 15cm (6in) tall. Use a hand fork to lightly prise them out of the ground, being careful not to disturb the remaining plants in the row.

◆ **SOW SEEDS** in regular batches for a prolonged harvest.

Storing & Using

They can be added to: salads...stir-fries...Asian dishes...sauces...mash...

Spring onions don't store well, so only lift them when you need them. You can keep them in the fridge for a few days but they will soon spoil – they cannot be frozen. Spring onions are delicious chopped into salads and provide a more delicate flavour than ordinary onions in a wide range of dishes.

Routine care

Spring onions are relatively trouble-free and very simple to grow. For a constant supply throughout summer, sow seeds every two weeks. They can also be grown through autumn and winter under cloches and fleece, and even on windowsills. If you have a greenhouse, sow seeds into large containers, and enjoy a year-round supply.

Thinning out When seedlings are 7.5cm (3in) tall, thin out every other plant in the row to leave them spaced 2cm (¾in) apart.

Weeding Remove weeds regularly from around the seedlings to prevent them competing for nutrients.

Watering Water regularly, and feed using a general-purpose liquid fertilizer as the plants mature.

spring onion

Project
Onion & garlic drying rack

It is crucial that harvested onions and garlic have an opportunity to dry out in the sun and fresh air before you store them, then they will keep for longer. A drying rack will ensure that air can circulate freely around the produce and any dry soil can fall off.

step **3**

MATERIALS & TOOLS
- timber, screwdriver, wire mesh, 8 L-shaped brackets, screws, hammer, staples

A work bench, clamps and a cordless screwdriver make the job easier. You can also work on an old table.

step **2**

Hammer the staples home along one side of the frame first, then pull the wire mesh taut before attaching the staples on the opposite side. Finish by attaching the mesh to the remaining two sides.

step **1**

Galvanised L-shaped brackets make quick work of assembling the basic framework. Screw one bracket to each face of the corners using countersunk screws.

1 Start by making the frame that will support the wire mesh. Connect the four pieces of the frame using flat L-shaped brackets screwed into place.

2 Screw uprights to the sides and front edge of the frame to strengthen it and prevent the onions from falling off. The back edge will be fixed to a fence.

3 Lay the wire mesh on the frame and secure it to all four sides with galvanised staples spaced approximately 20cm (8in) apart.

4 Hold the frame with its back edge against the fence and secure one corner through a fence post and the other through the fence rail with heavy-gauge screws.

step 4

Use a timber brace to hold the frame at the right height while you attach it to the fence. It can be removed after the front supporting legs are in place.

No fence

If you don't have a convenient fence or shed for supporting the rack, it will need four legs rather than two. Attach a diagonal timber brace between each pair of legs to help keep the rack stable.

step 5

Make a small hole in the ground for each support before driving it in fully. This makes the job of getting the supports in the ground easier.

5   Drive a support into the ground at each front corner of the rack along the sides. With the rack perfectly level, screw the supports into place.

Always spread out your produce in a single layer so that the air can circulate through it more efficiently. Turning the produce periodically will also speed up the drying process.

Florence fennel & Kohl rabi

These slightly unusual vegetables are harvested for their swollen stems, and are very easy to grow. Florence fennel has a mild aniseed flavour, and is often used in stir fries. Kohl rabi is part of the cabbage family, and has a mild, cabbage-like flavour. Both crops can be picked young and tender or left to grow for a more substantial harvest.

Timing Low temperatures can cause both crops, especially Florence fennel, to bolt, so don't sow them too early. Wait until the coldest period has passed.

Sowing

◆ **TO SOW UNDER COVER,** sow two or three seeds into small pots during spring, then thin the seedlings when they are about 5cm (2in) tall to leave the strongest plant per pot. Plant them out in late spring, leaving 25cm (10in) between each kohl rabi plant; 30cm (12in) between the Florence fennel. Plants will require hardening off for a few days prior to planting out by putting them outside during the day, then bringing them back inside at night.

◆ **TO SOW OUTSIDE,** sow kohl rabi from early spring, Florence fennel from late spring, into drills 2cm (¾in) deep. Sow the seed in small clusters, spacing the kohl rabi 25cm (10in) apart, and the Florence fennel 30cm (12in) apart. When the seedlings emerge, thin them out to leave the strongest plant per cluster.

Fennel tips

Take care not to confuse Florence fennel with the aromatic, leafy herb also called fennel. Florence fennel is an attractive plant to grow on the allotment, and will develop quickly if given fertile, well-drained soil. Keep the area around the crop free from weeds that would compete for moisture and nutrients, and may smother young plants.

Watering Water the plants regularly during the summer, and feed using a liquid fertilizer to promote strong growth.

Earthing up To blanch the stems and give them a sweeter flavour, pile earth up around the bulbs during summer.

Harvesting Harvest the stems by cutting through the base with a sharp knife. Plants can also be lifted whole and trimmed later.

Harvesting

The swollen stems of kohl rabi will take about 10 weeks until they are ready for picking, and should be no larger than a tennis ball. They should be cut at the base, at ground level, using a sharp knife. Florence fennel can be harvested at a younger stage, producing bulbs just 4–5cm (1½–2in) across in size, or full-size, when about 15cm (6in) across.

◆ **IF HARVESTING** in early summer, leave the stumps of Florence fennel in the ground and water them well. They will often re-sprout, providing more mini bulbs for the remainder of the growing season.

◆ **AFTER HARVESTING** kohl rabi, pull the roots from the soil and prepare the area for another crop.

Storing & Using

Florence fennel can be used in: gratin dishes...salads...soups...
Kohl rabi can be used in: stews...soups...salads...stir-fries...

Both Florence fennel and kohl rabi can be stored in the fridge for a few days, or can be chopped, blanched, then frozen for up to 6 months. Florence fennel is good with cheese or fish, and can be eaten raw. Kohl rabi is lightly flavoured and can be added to soups, stews, and stir-fries, or steamed as a side dish. The leaves can be eaten, too.

Florence fennel

white kohl rabi

Kohl rabi tips

Being part of the cabbage family, kohl rabi prefers heavy, rich soil that has been improved with plenty of organic matter. However, it is more tolerant of poorer soil conditions than many of the other cabbage members.

Cover up Watch out for pests, such as cabbage white butterflies and pigeons, that will quickly destroy the crop.

Weeding Remove competing weeds by hand, being careful not to disturb the swelling stems of the plant.

Harvesting Harvest the stems as soon as they are ready. Stems left too long become tough and inedible.

Celeriac & Parsnips

These two essential winter staples are perfect for supplying the kitchen with vegetables when the allotment is at its least productive. Celeriac has a mild, nutty flavour and one of its main virtues is its longevity in storage. Parsnips will benefit from exposure to the frost before harvesting, as this makes them sweeter.

Sowing celeriac

Celeriac needs a long growing season in order for the stems to mature fully, so seeds should be started off under cover in early spring.

Planting out Harden the seedlings off once they reach a good size and plant them outside into their final positions. Water them in well.

Watering Give the plants plenty of water and don't let the soil dry out. Celeriac grows best in very moist soil.

Growing

◆ **CELERIAC IS OFTEN** thought of as a root crop, yet it is the large, swollen stems that are eaten. To produce these, celeriac should be sown in early spring in small pots under cover, and planted out in late spring or early summer. Plant the seedlings 30cm (12in) apart and keep the centres of the plants just above the surface. It is an easy crop to grow, not minding sun or shade, although it does require a fertile soil.

◆ **PARSNIPS REQUIRE** a sunny open site, and soil that has been dug deeply to allow the tap roots to develop and grow. Alternatively, grow them in a raised bed, where you can provide the deep, free-draining, stone-less soil they need. Seeds should be sown directly into the soil in shallow drills. Once the seedlings emerge they should be thinned out to 10–20cm (4–8in) apart, depending on the size of parsnip roots required.

Celeriac Remove offshoots from celeriac as soon as you see them, as these will compete with the main plant for nutrients.

celeriac

Growing tips

Parsnips and celeriac can be damaged by carrot root fly burrowing into the roots. On allotments with bad infestations it is best to create a barrier to prevent the low-flying pests from landing and laying their eggs. Parsnip canker is a fungal disease causing black growths on the roots. Remove and dispose of infected plants immediately.

Seedlings Thin out parsnip seedlings when they emerge. Be patient, the seed can be very slow to germinate.

Watering Keep the plants well watered, particularly when they are young, as they can quickly wilt and die.

Carrot fly Watch out for carrot root flies on celeriac and parsnips. Erect a mesh barrier to protect the plants from attack.

Routine care

Since celeriac likes moist conditions, it will benefit from a thick layer of mulch placed around the plants in summer. Take care to keep it away from the stems. Regularly hand-weed around plants, water regularly, and occasionally give them a liquid feed.

◆ **IF YOU DON'T** require the space for planting something else on the allotment, it is best to only harvest parsnips and celeriac as and when they're needed, as they keep better when left in the ground. Both vegetables should be ready for harvesting from autumn and well into the winter months.

◆ **TO HARVEST** either vegetable, place a fork underneath the plant and gently prise it out of the ground. Be careful with parsnips as the long taproot can easily snap, particularly on heavy soil.

parsnips

Storing & Using

They can be used in: stews...mash...to make crisps...

Both vegetables will store in the fridge for a few days but are best pulled as and when you need them. Parsnips are a must for roast dinners, and celeriac mash with garlic and cream is delicious.

Parsnip crisps For delicious, home-made nibbles to serve with drinks, deep-fry thinly sliced parsnip, drain on kitchen paper, and season with salt.

Parsnips in sand Remove the tops of the parsnips, bury the root in moist sand and keep in a cool place, such as a shed or garage. They will store for 6 months.

Swedes & Turnips

Turnips must be one of the most versatile vegetables in the kitchen and can be grown not just for their delicious roots, but also for their leaves, which can be used like a cut-and-come-again salad. Sweet-tasting swedes are perfect for providing a delicious vegetable for winter roast dinners, when there is very little else growing on the allotment.

turnip 'Purple Top Milan'

swede 'Airlie'

swede 'Ruby'

Swede tips

Prior to sowing, prepare the soil thoroughly by digging in plenty of well-rotted organic matter, such as garden compost. Remove any large stones that could cause the roots to fork, and rake the soil surface level.

Thinning To produce full-size roots, swede seedlings should be thinned. This can be done gradually, always leaving the strongest seedlings to remain.

Protection Cover the seedlings over with fine mesh to prevent pests, such as cabbage white butterflies and pigeons, from attacking the crop.

Growing

◆ **SWEDES ARE** sown directly in the soil to allow them to develop their roots without disturbance, from mid-spring to midsummer. They are particularly slow-growing, taking about five months from sowing to harvest. Sow the seeds thinly, 2cm (¾in) deep, in rows spaced 38cm (15in) apart. Thin out the seedlings as they develop to a spacing of 23cm (9in) apart.

◆ **TURNIPS CAN** be sown directly outdoors (see right), but can also be started under cover to extend the growing season. Fill small pots with compost, water well, and then sow two or three seeds in each, 2cm (¾in) deep. When the seedlings emerge, thin them to leave the strongest plants per pot. Harden them off in a porch or cold frame before planting them out, 10cm (4in) apart, with 30cm (12in) between each row.

Routine care

Water seedlings regularly to encourage the roots to swell – if the soil dries out it can cause them to split. Turnips and swedes can be prone to flea beetle, so protect plants with fine mesh to prevent them from being damaged. Early-sown plants will need to be protected with a fleece if cold weather is predicted.

- ◆ **BABY TURNIPS** are ready to harvest in as little as six weeks, and should be carefully pulled when they reach the size of a golf ball. The small roots are tender and sweet.
- ◆ **FULL-SIZE TURNIPS** can take up to 35 weeks to mature, depending on variety, and are ready when the foliage starts to die back. To crop over a long period, harvest some young, leaving the rest to mature fully.
- ◆ **CHECK THE SOIL** pH if growing swedes, as they are prone to clubroot, which is less prevalent in alkaline soil.
- ◆ **TENDER TURNIP** varieties will not survive the winter, so make sure they have all been lifted before the temperatures drop.

turnip 'Oasis'

Storing & Using

They can be used in soups... stews...mash...or can be boiled...or roasted...

Turnips and swedes will keep in the fridge for a week. Alternatively, dice, blanch and freeze the roots, or cook, mash and then freeze. When frozen, both will keep for up to 9 months. Swede is traditionally served as mash, but like parsnips, it is also delicious roasted in the oven with herbs.

Swede mash
Boil and mash swede with butter, a little salt and some freshly ground black pepper.

Turnip soup
Turnips make a useful addition to soups, providing a mild flavour and lots of substance. Top with crunchy fried pancetta.

Turnip tips

If you want to grow turnips for their young, tender leaves, harvest the foliage every few weeks from mid- to late spring. The plants will still form small roots, but they are slower to develop. When harvesting turnips grown only for their roots, lift them when they reach your preferred size. Hardy varieties can be left in the soil until needed, even throughout winter.

Sowing seeds Turnips should be sown outdoors in spring into drills, 2cm (¾in) deep, spaced 20cm (8in) apart.

Weeding Regularly hand weed among the emerging seedlings, taking care not to disturb the developing roots.

Harvesting Harvest young turnips during the summer to enjoy their delicious flavour and succulent texture.

Beetroots

One of the most colourful root vegetables to grow, beetroots are reliable and relatively trouble free. They are best known for its round red roots, although there are also yellow-, white-, and stripy-fleshed varieties – with slender, stumpy, or fat roots. All taste delicious, especially when roasted to bring out their natural sweetness, and, of course, when they are pickled.

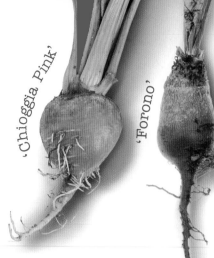

'Chioggia Pink'

'Forono'

Sowing inside

Sowing beetroots indoors gives them a head start as long as they are planted out before their roots fill their pots or modules. Sow from late winter.

Thinning Sow one seed in each pot or module. If more than one seedling germinates, then thin them out to the strongest one.

Planting Plant out the seedlings at a spacing of 10cm (4in) between each plant, taking care not to cause any disturbance to the roots.

Growing

Beetroots require a moist, fertile, well-drained soil, and can be grown in sun or light shade. Avoid growing them in stony soil, which can cause the roots to split. Unusually, the "seed" of most varieties is more like a capsule, and usually contains three or four true seeds. Thin the seedlings after sowing.

◆ **BEETROOTS CAN** be prone to bolting if sown too early, meaning that they run to seed. To avoid the risk when sowing outdoors in spring, choose bolt-resistant varieties such 'Boltardy'.

◆ **ON SMALLER PLOTS** consider growing beetroots in large containers and harvest them while young and tender.

Sowing outside

Seeds can be sown directly outside from spring to midsummer. Prepare the soil before sowing by digging it over, removing any weeds and stones, then rake the surface level. The seeds are large, so are easy to space out in drills.

Sowing Create a shallow drill, water it well, sow seeds at 10cm (4in) intervals.

Thinning One seed can produce many seedlings so thin out to leave the strongest.

'Cheltenham Green Top'

'Red Ace'

'Boltardy'

Growing tips

Beetroots require little attention through the season. However, a few routine jobs are worth doing.

Weeding Regularly hand weed between the seedlings to stop weeds from competing for moisture, taking care not to damage the roots.

Watering When watering, direct the flow to the base of the plants. Avoid wetting the leaves as this can encourage diseases to spread.

Harvesting Pick your beetroots while they are young, and eat them immediately to enjoy their tenderness and delicious flavour.

Routine care

Beetroot plants will tolerate drought but they produce more succulent roots if watered well during dry spells. Don't overwater them, however, as this can encourage leaves to grow at the expense of the roots.

◆ **SOW REGULARLY** every two or three weeks throughout spring and midsummer to ensure a constant supply.

◆ **IN DRY SUMMERS**, mulch around plants to retain moisture.

◆ **HARVEST BEETROOTS** about 12 weeks after sowing, although this depends on the variety. The roots taste at their best when dug up young and tender. Use a hand fork to gently prise the roots out of the ground.

Storing & Using

They can be used in soups...salads... or can be roasted...or pickled...

Surplus roots can be stored in layers in wooden boxes lined with newspaper and filled with sand. Young beetroots can be frozen. Boil them until tender, slice or cube, then freeze for up to 6 months.

Soup Beetroot soup, or borscht, can be made in a variety of ways. In some countries it is traditional to add bacon or other meats, in others yogurt or soured cream is added.

Pickled Dice or slice beetroot for pickling and put in sterilized jars with vinegar, garlic, and bay leaves. It will keep for up to a year.

Radishes

One of the fastest and easiest of the salad crops to grow, radishes are perfect for beginners as they take just a few weeks from sowing to harvesting. They're ideal for filling small gaps on the allotment, and can be sown alongside other, slower-maturing crops.

Continuous crops Sow summer radishes little and often in spring and summer for a continuous supply of delicious, crunchy roots.

Sowing outdoors

Prepare the soil before sowing, digging it over to remove any weeds or stones, then rake it level. Sow the seeds directly in the soil, in spring and summer for summer radishes, and late summer for winter varieties.

Preparing drills Create drills 1cm (½in) deep, spacing them 15cm (6in) apart for summer radishes, and 25cm (10in) apart for winter types.

Watering the seeds Before sowing, water the drills, then sow the seeds about 1cm (½in) apart. Thin out excess seedlings as they emerge.

Growing

Choose between the two main types of radishes. Traditional summer radishes are very fast-growing, and can be sown and harvested from spring to autumn. Winter and oriental (mooli) radishes produce larger roots than summer-types, and are sown in late summer, ready to harvest from mid-autumn to spring.

◆ **YOU DON'T** have to wait long to be harvesting these delicious crunchy vegetables. Summer radishes take as little as three to six weeks between sowing and picking. Winter radishes are slower to mature but they are well worth the wait.

◆ **DON'T LEAVE SUMMER** radishes in the ground for too long as they become woody, pithy, and inedible very quickly. Pick the radishes daily, checking along the row to find the largest roots. Pull them as soon as they are big enough.

radishes

Harvest Pull summer radishes out by hand or gently ease them out with a trowel. Large winter radishes should be lifted using a spade.

Jerusalem artichokes

Make sure you've got plenty of space on the allotment if you fancy growing these knobbly root vegetables. Harvested in autumn, these vigorous and tall perennials can also provide pretty yellow flowers in summer. Expensive to buy in the shops, growing Jerusalem artichokes is a cost-effective way to enjoy these sweetly succulent delicacies.

Flowers Jerusalem artichokes are related to sunflowers and can provide the allotment with an impressive floral display during the summer.

Growing

If you have poor soil and an area of shade on the allotment then don't despair, as Jerusalem artichokes will positively thrive in these conditions. They are the thugs of the vegetable world and will quickly swamp and shade out other plants if they're not kept in check. However, once you have tried these nutty-tasting tubers, you will agree that they are well worth including.

◆ **TUBERS SHOULD** be planted in early to mid-spring after digging over the soil and adding well-rotted manure or garden compost. They should be planted 15cm (6in) deep and 60cm (24in) apart. If you are growing more than one row, then space them 90cm (36in) apart.

◆ **THEY ARE** relatively trouble-free and should be harvested as and when they are required in autumn and winter. Harvest them as you do potatoes, by lifting with a garden fork.

Wind protection

Jerusalem artichokes are simple to grow but their tall, rampant habit can make them susceptible to wind damage. To help prevent this, mound the soil up around the base of each stem. Large clumps will withstand the wind better than individual plants.

Plant supports On exposed sites it may be necessary to help to prevent wind damage by using canes and strings for support.

Storing & Using

They can be used for: salads...or can be roasted...boiled...or braised in butter...

Tubers keep unwashed in the fridge for about 2 weeks, but are not suitable for freezing because they discolour and their texture deteriorates.

jerusalem artichokes

vegetables

stems

leeks • celery •
rhubarb • asparagus

Leeks

If you find onions strong and overpowering, try growing leeks for a milder flavour. Not only is this delicious vegetable easy to grow, but it is also an essential winter crop, providing flavoursome sustenance from autumn to early spring, when your choice of vegetables is more limited.

Sowing

To get leeks off to an early start, sow seeds under cover in a greenhouse or on a window ledge in midwinter.

Container sowing Lightly sprinkle seeds over moist seed compost in seed trays or recycled pots. Leeks don't mind having their roots disturbed so can easily be lifted and transplanted.

Trim the roots Before transplanting, give their roots a quick trim. This makes it easier to drop the seedlings in their planting holes.

Growing

Leeks are best grown in seed trays under cover (see left), then transplanted to their final positions when they are about 15–20cm (6–8in) high. Plant them out 25–30cm (8–12in) apart. They prefer full sun but will tolerate some light shade.

◆ **TO PLANT THEM OUT,** make holes 5cm (2in) wide and 15cm (6in) deep. Trim the roots (see left), leaving about 2.5cm (1in), then drop the plants into the holes. Don't push the soil back but instead water them in (see below), allowing the soil to crumble naturally around the plants. This allows space for the stems to swell.

◆ **MOUND SOIL** around the base as the leeks grow. The mounding is what will produce the blanched, white stems.

Puddle planting When planting young leeks out, make a hole and drop a plant in. Don't replace the soil but instead water well to create a puddle around the plant.

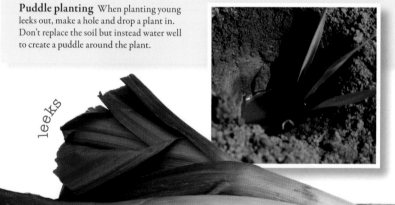

leeks

Celery

Traditionally, celery was considered one of the trickier crops to grow. It had to be planted out in a deep trench with the soil earthed up to keep the sun off the developing stems. This ensured nice white sticks of celery. Today's self-blanching varieties do the same job with far less bother.

Seedlings Once the seedlings are big enough, they can be transferred to individual pots to grow on.

Growing

Although some consider the old, trenching varieties of celery to have a better flavour, beginners are advised to avoid them. After sowing under cover, plant out self-blanching seedlings 23cm (9in) apart in blocks (see below). Harden the plants off before planting out in well-prepared soil containing plenty of well-rotted organic matter, to help the soil retain moisture.

◆ **USE CARDBOARD** to wrap the stems on the outside of the blocks as they emerge from the soil. This will prevent the sun from reaching the stems and turning them green.

◆ **HARVEST FROM** August onwards, making sure your crop is all in before the first frosts arrive.

Storing & Using

It can be used in: salads... soups...casseroles... stuffings...stir-fries...

Good-quality, fresh celery is a treat. It can be stored in the salad crisper compartment of the fridge for a week or so and eaten with cheese or in a Waldorf salad, where it is one of the essential ingredients. Alternatively, you can cut celery into pieces, blanch it and freeze it for up to 9 months, but it goes mushy when defrosted, so frozen celery is best used to make soups or casseroles. Once made, these can be frozen if required.

celery

Growing tips

Celery requires a long growing season so start it off indoors in early to mid-spring, scattering the seeds lightly on a seed tray of moist compost. They require light to germinate, so cover them with a minimal amount of compost, if any. Place in a heated propagator and pot up individually when they emerge. Plant them out when they are 15cm (6in) tall.

Plant in blocks Plant self-blanching varieties in a close grid. This will prevent the sunlight from reaching the stems.

Harvest carefully Celery lasts better if you keep the root intact when you harvest. Cut stems rapidly turn brown.

Rhubarb

This traditional allotment perennial will reward you with a bumper crop of brightly coloured red or pink stems from late spring to midsummer. Rhubarb is a hungry, luxuriant plant, so feed and water it well to keep it healthy and cropping abundantly year after year.

Growing

Rhubarb requires a rich, heavy soil, so prepare the planting area well by digging it over, and incorporating lots of rotted manure or garden compost. It is a large, long-lived, perennial plant so consider the long-term when deciding where to plant it.

◆ **HARVEST REPEATEDLY** in spring and summer by pulling and twisting the stems upwards. Don't pick after midsummer to give the plant time to recover, ready for next year's crop. Stems that grow in late summer are also tough.

◆ **LARGE PLANTS** should be divided in autumn to encourage healthy growth, and to prevent the centre becoming woody. Only keep strong, healthy sections and discard the rest.

rhubarb 'Victoria'

Storing & Using

It can be used in: jam...compote...crumble... cakes...pastries...pickles...or can be frozen...

Cut stems will keep in the fridge for a few days, and last longer with their leaves still attached. The stems can also be sliced and blanched before freezing, and will last for 6 months. Always discard the leaves, which are poisonous.

Jam Rhubarb is often combined with ginger to produce a beautiful, jewel-like, pink jam.

Growing tips

Buy rhubarb as a young plant but don't crop the stems for the first year to help it establish quicker. Plant new plants from autumn to spring. Rhubarb can tolerate some shade, which is a good way to make use of these areas.

Forcing Stems can be forced by placing a cover over the plant in winter. The first stems produced are very sweet and tender.

Mulching Rhubarb should be mulched with organic matter each year in spring to help retain moisture in the soil.

Harvesting Pick stems every couple of weeks until midsummer. Leave some leaves each time, so the plant can grow.

Asparagus

This is a fine example of patience being a virtue as you can't harvest asparagus spears for the first two or three years after planting. However, once you have tasted these delicate spears smothered in melted butter, you will realize that it was well worth the wait.

Growing

The most popular way of growing asparagus is by planting "crowns", which are young plants, usually sold bare rooted. It is a long-term crop, and may grow in the same bed for up to 15 years, so prepare the soil thoroughly before planting. Remove any perennial weeds, and dig in plenty of well-rotted compost.

- ◆ **ASPARAGUS PREFERS** light, fertile, and well-drained soil. If the soil on your allotment is poor, then consider growing it in raised beds.
- ◆ **HARVEST SPEARS** in the third year after planting, using a knife to cut the stems just below soil level when they are 20cm (8in) tall.

Storing & Using

It can be used in: tarts...risottos...flans...or can be boiled...or steamed...

The spears can be stored in the fridge for a few days by standing their bases in a glass of water, refreshing it daily. To freeze, trim the spears and briefly blanch them first. They can be frozen whole or chopped. One of the best ways to eat the new season's spears is steamed with melted butter, lemon juice, and freshly ground black pepper. They also go well with chicken, salmon, and pork.

Tart Crisp shortcrust pastry, free-range eggs, mature cheddar, and asparagus spears make this tart a special treat.

Growing tips

Asparagus is easy to grow but check for bright red asparagus beetles that can damage and kill the stems. Pick them off or use a suitable insecticide. The ferny growth may need staking during summer, before dying back in the autumn.

Planting Plant asparagus crowns 30cm (12in) apart. They are often planted in trenches with a mound in the bottom to sit on.

Harvesting The spears can be cut for about 10 weeks, after which they should be allowed to grow to keep the plant strong.

Care Remove the attractive ferny growth at the end of each year, when it starts to turn yellow and die back.

vegetables

herbs

annual & perennial herbs
• shrubby herbs

Annual & Perennial herbs

You can grow a wide range of annual and perennial herbs to add scent to the allotment and flavour to your home cooking. Not only do many herbs look attractive, but an added bonus is that there are numerous ways of storing your home-grown herbs for future use. You will never need to buy expensive, short-lived supermarket herbs again.

basil

Growing parsley

Parsley can be bought from garden centres, but the quality is better if you sow your own. Sow the seeds directly in late spring and then every few weeks during summer for a continuous crop. Cover plants with a cloche for overwintering.

Pest attack Watch out for carrot root fly; parsley and carrots are related hence both can be attacked by this pest.

Annuals

Annual herbs are easy to grow from seed and you can get a good crop even from a small space.

◆ **CORIANDER** that is grown for its leaves does best in partial shade. Sow it directly outdoors in spring and harvest it when the leaves are young and fresh. Use them in Middle-Eastern and Asian cooking.

◆ **BORAGE** is a stunning annual herb whose leaves have a mild cucumber flavour and can be added to salads. Be warned, it is a prolific self-seeder, so make sure you really want to grow it.

◆ **BASIL** is a half-hardy, scented herb that is grown as an annual and is often associated with Italian cuisine. Sow the seeds directly outdoors in late spring. Try growing the purple-leaved variety to add colour to your allotment plot.

◆ **PARSLEY** is a popular annual that is technically a biannual, but is treated as an annual. Flat-leaved, or French, parsley has a stronger flavour, while curly-leaved, or common, parsley is more compact.

parsley

dill

coriander

golden marjoram

Perennials

From low-growing creepers to large shrubs, perennial herbs look good growing in their own dedicated bed in the allotment or dotted among other plants.

♦ **CHIVES** produce beautiful purple flowers and are perfect as a border around beds or for underplanting fruit trees. Plant them near carrots; their pungent smell (they are part of the onion family) confuses the carrot root fly and reduces attacks.

♦ **TARRAGON** is a hardy perennial with upright branched stems. It is traditionally used to flavour chicken dishes and sauces.

♦ **FENNEL** is a tall, attractive perennial with ferny aniseed-flavoured foliage that is a welcome addition to the herb garden.

Growing mint

There are more than 120 varieties of mint to try, including chocolate, ginger and orange mint. All mint is extremely vigorous though, so you should plant it in a pot in the ground to prevent it from taking over.

Storing & Using

They can be used in: soups...stews...risottos...drinks...bread...pasta dishes... herb teas... or frozen...or dried...or in home remedies...

Fresh herbs store well for up to 10 days wrapped in damp kitchen paper in an open plastic bag in the fridge. The leaves also freeze well (remove them from the stems first). Alternatively, air-drying is a good way to preserve herbs with minimal loss of flavour and quality.

Bouquet garni
This is a bundle of herbs tied in a muslin bag or with string and used to flavour casseroles, stocks, sauces and soups. It is discarded before serving the dish.

Air-drying fennel This is an excellent way to preserve fennel fronds for use in soups, sauces and salad dressings throughout the year.

Comfrey fertilizer Comfrey is the ideal herb to grow if you want to produce a high-nutrient feed for plants such as tomatoes (see p.58).

chives

marjoram

tarragon

lovage

mint

Shrubby herbs

Many shrubby herbs are evergreen and will provide year-round interest for your plot. Individual plants such as bay or rosemary can be used as focal points for the centre of parterres and vegetable beds, while lavender and sage look – and smell – terrific when edging pathways and planted around seating areas.

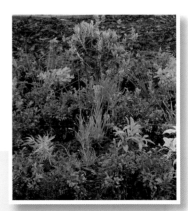

Herb parterre (see p.86) A shrubby lavender plant takes centre stage in a herb-filled parterre edged with low, tightly clipped evergreen hedges.

Herb lawns

The creeping habit of both thyme and chamomile make them ideal for creating areas of scented herbal lawn. Avoid walking on them too often, since they can wear quickly.

Scented lawn Plant small specimens 25cm (10in) apart into well-drained soil and they will quickly knit together to make an evergreen carpet.

In the ground

Most shrubby herbs thrive in light, well-drained soil. If your plot suffers from heavy soil, then dig in plenty of horticultural grit to counteract this.

Be aware that many shrubby herbs can get large and quickly outgrow their space if they are not clipped regularly.

◆ **TRAIN BAY** as a standard or pyramid to create a focal point in the allotment. Alternatively, leave it to grow into a bush to screen unsightly areas such as the compost heap.

◆ **USE ROSEMARY** as hedging; some varieties can get quite large. Similarly, rows of lavender can be used as low-growing hedging to give a formal structure to the plot and attract bees.

◆ **PURPLE AND TRICOLOUR SAGE** add a splash of colour and make an attractive feature for any plot. Hyssop, lavender and rosemary all produce beautiful flowers, which add an extra ornamental quality to any space.

thyme

purple sage

green sage

Useful fillers

Herbs are extremely versatile and as they don't require a lot of nutrients, they can be slotted into spaces that are unsuitable for other plants. Use small herbs such as thyme and chamomile dotted along the edges of paths or even in the gaps between paving slabs.

Keep compact Lavenders can be kept compact by clipping twice a year so they can fit into small spaces.

Fill the gaps Thyme plants can be used to fill tiny gaps in paths and at the edges, where it will slowly spread.

Storing & Using

They can be used in: stocks...soups...fish dishes... or dried...or frozen...

Since rosemary and bay are both evergreen, you can pick the leaves as and when you need them. You can also preserve shrubby herbs by air-drying them. Tie them in small bundles and hang them up in a cool, dry place. When they are completely dry, store them in an airtight container. They will retain more flavour if you store them whole and crush the leaves when you are ready to use them. Dried herbs are best used within a year. As a guide, use one teaspoon of crumbled dried leaves in place of one tablespoon of fresh herbs.

In pots

Herbs thrive in pots and these can be moved around as your design evolves, for example to provide an instant focal point. They don't need as much watering or feeding as most plants in pots, but should be checked regularly throughout the summer.

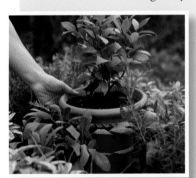

- **PLANT A SELECTION** of herbs in the individual planting holes of a strawberry pot.
- **MOVE HERBS IN POTS** to a shady area to prevent them drying out when you go on holiday.

Containers Herbs in terracotta pots make both beautiful and practical features in the veggie garden.

Soap Herbal soaps are easy to make with dried herbs and make great gifts for friends and family.

Oils and vinegars Add sprigs of herbs to oils and vinegars to make excellent infusions at a fraction of the price of those on sale in the shops.

hyssop

rosemary

bay

FRUIT

Growing & Storing

fruit

soft

strawberries • a fruit cage • raspberries • a raspberry cane support • blueberries & cranberries • a sunken blueberry bed • blackberries & hybrids • gooseberries • currants

Strawberries

These are the nation's favourite fruit, and as the plants need little space and fruit freely, they are ideal for smaller plots. They can be grown in hanging baskets from the allotment shed, or in troughs and containers. Grow them in a raised bed to save on backbreaking weeding, and to make it easier to pick the soft, succulent, summer berries.

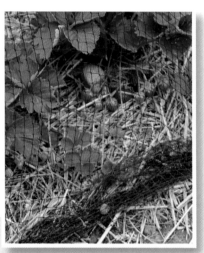

Netting Birds love these juicy fruits so make sure you cover the plants early on with a net to protect them.

Planting

Dig over the plot thoroughly, removing all weeds, and add plenty of organic matter to the soil before planting. The best time to plant strawberries is late summer, while the soil is still warm. Water them in well after planting.

Spacing Plant strawberries using a trowel, spacing them 45cm (18in) apart, in rows 1m (3ft) apart.

Growing

Grow strawberries in well-drained but fertile soil, in a sunny, sheltered location. If you have poor soil, grow them in raised beds or containers instead. Always buy certified virus-free plants, and avoid planting in soil that has previously been used to grow potatoes or tomatoes. These crops are prone to the disease verticillium wilt, which can be passed to the strawberries.

◆ **STRAWBERRIES** establish better when planted in late summer, and will give a small crop the following summer. They can be planted in spring, although their first year's flowers should be removed to help them root better. Water new plants well.

◆ **GROW A MIX** of early- and late-season summer-fruiting varieties for sweet-tasting fruit from late May through to mid-July. Perpetual strawberries crop from midsummer to autumn, although they aren't as tasty as summer varieties.

alpine strawberries

strawberries

Propagating

Strawberries constantly produce "runners", which are new shoots bearing new plants, making them one of the easiest plants to propagate. Peg the young plants into small pots of compost plunged into the soil. Keep them well watered, and after a few weeks, the stem between the new and old plant can be cut. If you don't want new plants, remove the runners to prevent them competing for nutrients.

Anchor When a runner is sent out from the main plant, peg it into a pot of compost to encourage it to root quickly. It can be plant out once large enough.

◆ **IF YOU WANT** a constant supply of new plants, grow a few strawberry plants in a dedicated bed. Allow them to form runners and plant them out when large enough.

Fruit protection

One of the key jobs when growing strawberries is preventing the fruit from coming into contact with the soil and rotting. There are various methods of stopping this from happening.

Plastic sheeting Planting through plastic sheeting or landscape fabric prevents the berries rotting and also suppresses weeds.

Collars These are placed around the plants, keeping the fruits off the soil. They can either be bought, or you can make your own using cardboard.

Straw This is the traditional method, hence the name "strawberries". Barley straw is the best type to use as it is soft and pliable. Buy it at pet shops.

Storing & Using

They can be used in: Eton Mess...summer puddings...strawberries & cream...strawberry daiquiri...tarts...milk shakes...ice cream...jam ...Pimms...or can be frozen...

Eating your first bowl of strawberries with cream is the perfect way to celebrate the arrival of summer. Freshly picked strawberries don't keep for long in the fridge – a day or two at the most. Freeze for up to 12 months, although the fruits go mushy when defrosted and are best used for jam-making or smoothies.

Jam A glut of strawberries can be put to good use in making a supply of jam for the store cupboard.

Summer pudding This quintessentially British pudding is easy to make, and is delicious served with ice cream.

Strawberry tart Make or buy a tart case and fill with strawberries and other summer berries for a quick and easy dessert.

Milk shakes Fresh strawberries make the best milk shake ever. Combine with ice chips to make a slush drink.

Project
Fruit cage

It's important to protect the tasty fruits and vegetables that you've spent weeks striving to grow on your allotment. Birds and small animals are unbelievably adept at knowing exactly when the time is right to steal your crops, so keep them at bay by making this simple protective cage.

step **3**

step **2**

MATERIALS & TOOLS
- bamboo canes or dowelling in various lengths, cane joiners, garden netting, wire staples

To maintain a rigid structure that will withstand the rigours of repeated removal of the netting when you harvest your produce, do not space the canes more than 1.2m (4ft) apart.

The holes in the cane joiners should match the diameter of your canes; the canes should fit snugly, not tightly.

step **1**

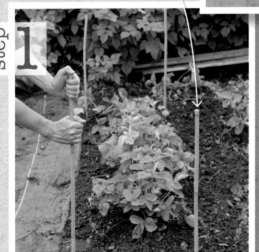

1 Drive four equal lengths of bamboo cane into the ground at a depth of about 20cm (8in) at each corner around the plant or plants to be protected.

2 Slide a ball-shaped cane joiner on top of each cane. Most cane joiners have multiple holes so you can make a simple frame, as here, or join several canes in a straight line to make a frame with longer sides.

3 Complete the assembly of the canes, leaving enough room around the plant so that the netting, once it is in place, does not snag the plant.

4 Drape the garden netting over the structure, ensuring there is enough netting to enable you to peg it into the ground all the way around the cage.

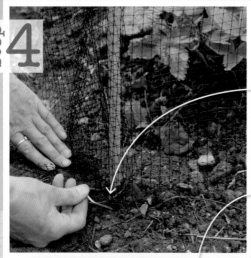

step 4

Wire staples, bent pieces of wire or short lengths of cane are perfect for holding the netting in place. The key point is that they can easily be removed.

Use small-gauge mesh to deter birds and make sure you replace it properly each time you access the cage.

Other systems

For bigger fruit and vegetable cages to protect established plants or bushes, there are plenty of alternatives to choose from. Some you can construct to suit your own specific requirements, using off-the-shelf components – aluminium tubing, frame connectors and netting of the appropriate gauge. Others, such as fruit-tree cages, only require assembly. These alternatives are durable and long-lasting.

This large cage is made from bought components. Instead of removing the netting for harvesting, you can lift it up or cut a hole in it and tie it back together.

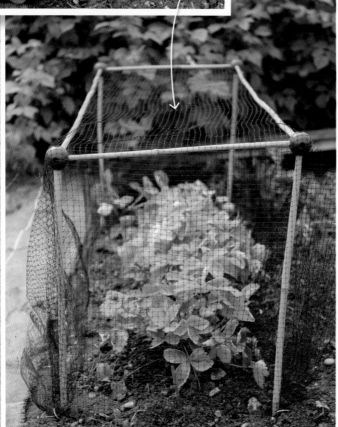

This simple fruit cage leaves the plant or bush with ample room for further growth upwards and sideways. Make sure that the netting is held taut over the top and along the sides to prevent birds from becoming entangled in it.

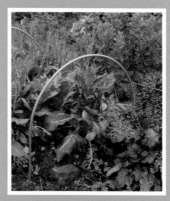

Metal hoops can be inserted into the ground in a row to protect plants that do not grow too high. Drape netting over the top of the row to form a tunnel.

Raspberries

Raspberries are relatively expensive to buy, but are very easy to grow and
don't need a lot of space, which makes growing your own a good idea.
They are one of the first berry fruits to crop each year, and taste wonderful
when picked fresh. There are summer- and autumn-fruiting varieties, which
means you could be picking delicious fruits from midsummer to the first frosts.

'Tulameen'

Raspberry canes

Raspberries can either be
bought growing in containers,
often with several plants per
pot, or as wrapped bundles
of bare-root canes (see below).

Buying Each plant comes as a single
cane, a bit thicker than a pencil, with its
own root system. Look for small white
buds from which new shoots will grow.

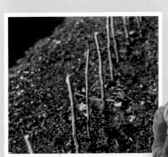

Planting Prepare the soil well in
advance with well-rotted compost
or manure, and erect post-and-wire
supports for summer-fruiting varieties.
Space the plants evenly and water well.

Growing

Choose a sheltered site, out of strong winds but in full sun, as
raspberries ripen best in these conditions. Plant container-grown
plants at any time of the year, but bare-root plants between late
autumn and early spring, unless the ground is frozen.

◆ **BEFORE PLANTING** the canes, dig a trench and add plenty
of well-rotted manure or compost and mix with the soil. This
helps to retain moisture.

◆ **SUMMER RASPBERRIES** require support, and should be
planted next to horizontal wires, stretched 40cm (16in) and
80cm (32in) above the soil, between sturdy posts (see p.196).

◆ **RASPBERRIES** should be spaced 35–45cm (14–18in) apart
and rows should be 1.2–2m (4–6ft) apart. They do not need
planting very deeply, about 7.5cm (3in) is sufficient.

'Octavia'

'All Gold'

Routine care

Raspberries like free-draining soil, but they also need plenty of water. They will tolerate a little shade, but need plenty of sunshine to give the best crop.

◆ **KEEP PLANTS** well watered during the summer and apply tomato feed to promote a good harvest. Mulch near the base of the canes to suppress weeds and retain moisture.

◆ **AS SOON AS** the fruit starts to ripen, protect it from birds. Cover the plants with netting, held taut using canes to prevent snaring unsuspecting birds, or a cage. Autumn-fruiting varieties seem to suffer less from attack by birds.

◆ **THE BERRIES** are ready to pick as soon as they turn fully red or yellow, depending on variety, and pull away easily from the plant leaving the central "plug" behind.

Careful picking Pull the fruits gently from the plants to avoid damaging them, as they will keep for much longer when the fruits are whole.

Pruning

Summer- and autumn-fruiting raspberries demand different pruning regimes.

Summer fruiting Old stems are pruned straight after the last fruits have been harvested, right down to the base. Leave younger stems and tie them in.

Autumn fruiting Prune in winter by cutting all stems down to the ground. New stems will appear in spring.

Storing & Using

They can be used for: jams...coulis...crumbles...tarts...puddings...or frozen...

Raspberry gluts are not to be greeted with despair. This fruit freezes incredibly well and can be used for lots of desserts, including summer puddings, flans and tarts, then, come the autumn and winter, spiced fruit compotes, fruit crumbles and mixed berry pies. If you don't have time to make jam when the fruit is ripe, simply freeze the berries and make the jam when you are less busy. Raspberries keep in the fridge for only a day or two, so are best eaten as soon as they are picked if you are not planning to freeze them.

Freezing Raspberries freeze very well, especially if frozen individually first by spacing them out on a tray. When they are frozen, they can be transferred to a plastic freezer bag and will not stick together, so you can use just a few at a time if you want.

Jam Raspberry jam is easy to make and there are dozens of recipes online. It will store for a year unopened. Once open, keep it in the fridge. Use it for bakewell tarts, jam tarts and sponge cake fillings.

Project
Raspberry cane support

Most raspberry varieties benefit from being grown against a support. A relatively simple structure consisting of sturdy posts with taut wires running between them, to which the canes can be tied in, not only supports the plants and keeps them tidy, but also makes pruning and harvesting the fruit much easier.

step 3

MATERIALS & TOOLS

- four stakes, galvanized wire, four straining bolts, galvanized clout nails
- sledgehammer, drill, pliers, saw

step 2

Secure the bracing post with a single 10cm (4in) galvanised clout nail and drill pilot holes slightly larger than the diameter of the straining bolts.

Cut each bracing post at a 90-degree angle and use the cut end to help determine the position of the notch.

step 1

Drive in a bracing post alongside each of the main posts. This will be angled so make sure that it will not obstruct the two supporting wires at the point where it will be attached to the main post.

1   Make two small holes in the soil approximately 40cm (16in) deep and your chosen distance apart, then hammer in the main supporting posts until they are completely firm in the ground.

2   Angle each bracing post, and where it crosses the main post mark the main post for the location of the notch.

3   Cut a notch into the main post to fit the bracing post snugly, then mark and drill holes 40cm (16in) and 80cm (31½in) from the bottom of the main post.

4   Push a straining bolt through each of the holes, fitting a washer and nut to the outside of each post.

step 4

Figure of eight

The canes can now be tied in to the supporting wires with twine to stop them from being blown over or snapping. Use a simple "figure of eight" – one loop of twine goes around the wire and the other around the stem of the plant. This method of tying in prevents rubbing but still allows enough room for the raspberry cane to grow.

step 5

5 Feed the galvanized wire through one bolt, use pliers to twist the cut end over the other, then feed the other end through its opposite bolt, maintaining a good tension.

6 Using pliers, tightly wrap the other end around the taut wire and press the cut end firmly in place so there are no sharp protrusions.

Using pliers, cut the other end of the galvanised wire to the correct length, allowing an extra 10cm (4in).

Tension each of the wires by tightening up the nuts on the straining bolts to take up any slack.

step 6

Position the raspberry cane support in a sunny or partly shaded location for best results. The support makes the task of picking the fruit much easier.

Blueberries & Cranberries

These closely related "super fruits" require moist, acid soil – cranberries especially prefer quite boggy soil. Few allotments are likely to offer these conditions but they can easily be provided by creating raised or sunken beds, filled with lime-free, ericaceous compost.

Netting Place nets over the fruit bushes as soon as they start to ripen to prevent birds from taking the fruit.

Growing

The first step before planting either fruit is to test the pH of your soil using a simple kit bought from a garden centre – see p.21, "Know your soil", for details how. Both fruits require a sunny site and should be kept moist at all times. They are usually sold pot-grown, and are best planted from autumn to spring.

◆ **BLUEBERRIES** are "self fertile", so you only need one plant to produce a crop. However, they fruit better if other varieties are grown nearby.

◆ **PRUNE** blueberries in early spring by removing one-third of the older wood at ground level.

◆ **WATER THE PLANTS** regularly using rainwater, for instance from a water butt. Most tap water is too alkaline for these acid-loving plants.

Suitable fertilizer Don't use traditional fertilizers when feeding blueberries and cranberries, as they can increase the soil's pH. Only use feeds designed for acid-loving plants.

Blueberry bed

These plants naturally grow on heath land, and require similar conditions if they are going to thrive on the allotment. Their two main requirements are moisture and acid soil. To achieve this, dig a 30cm (12in) deep pit, as large as you need, and line it with punctured pond liner. Fill the pit with lime-free, ericaceous compost, which is suitable for acid-loving plants.

Preparing to plant Take the blueberry plant out of its container and then tease the roots out gently.

Planting Dig a hole and plant the blueberry in it at the same depth as it was in the container. Firm it in and water well.

Mulching Mulch around the blueberry with well-rotted, acidic material, such as composted bark or pine needles.

Harvesting

Blueberries are ready for harvesting in midsummer, when they turn from greenish-white to deep blue. The attractive white bloom on the berries indicates that they are ready to pick. Cranberries ripen during autumn, turning deep, glossy red when they are ready (see right).

◆ RIPE BERRIES should easily detach from the plant but take care not to squash them. Damaged berries can't be stored.

◆ CHECK BUSHES regularly during summer, as the berries will ripen at different times on the same plant.

Picking fruit Pick the ripe berries individually, taking care not to dislodge any unripe ones.

Cranberries

These low-growing, creeping evergreen shrubs thrive in similar conditions to blueberries, requiring moist, acid soil. They produce their attractive red berries later than blueberries, in autumn.

Ripe berries Cranberries start to ripen in early autumn and keep well for a couple of months when left on the bush, unless eaten by birds first.

Storing & Using

Blueberries can be used in: pies...muffins...cookies...pancakes...
Cranberries can be used in: sauces...jellies...preserves...drinks...curds...or can be dried...

Make delicious blueberry pies and freeze them, or freeze the fruit in bags to use later. Cranberries freeze very well or can be dried. To dry them, pour boiling water over the berries to burst the skins, freeze them on a tray, then place them in a warm oven overnight.

Cranberry sauce Once you've made your own, you'll never buy it again. It freezes very well and will keep for 6 months at least.

Freezing Freeze berries on trays, then when they are completely frozen transfer them to freezer bags. Keep for up to 12 months.

Sunken planter An old ceramic sink can be filled with lime-free, ericaceous compost and kept moist, to make the ideal place for growing cranberries.

blueberries

cranberries

Project
Sunken blueberry bed

Blueberries are ericaceous plants, which means they must have acidic, lime-free soil. They also prefer soil that is free-draining but moisture-retentive. Unless your garden offers these conditions, the best way to grow a large number of blueberries is in a sunken bed, built in a sheltered, sunny or partly shaded site.

The frame should now sit level and square in the hole, and just proud of the soil surface. The excavated soil can be used later around the edges.

step **2**

step **1**

MATERIALS & TOOLS
- treated wooden planks and pegs
- landscape fabric, ericaceous compost

Mark out the perimeter of the frame on the soil surface using the edge of a spade or a pointed stick.

Cranberries

Blueberries require plenty of space between plants, up to 1.5m (5ft), depending on variety. To make full use of the bed, underplant the blueberries with cranberries, which also thrive in the ericaceous conditions. These dense, low-growing shrubs complement blueberries perfectly, and can bear surprisingly heavy crops.

1 Construct the frame of the bed in the same manner as the raised bed (see pp.38–39) and place it in position. Ensure the frame is square, using a Tee-square to check the angles, or by making sure that the diagonal measurements across the middle are equal.

2 Excavate the soil from within the outlines made (see above) and set it aside to use elsewhere. Dig down to a depth slightly less than the height of your timber frame, so that the frame sits proud of the surrounding soil.

3 Secure the frame by driving in a wooden peg at each corner to 10cm (4in) deeper than the depth of the frame. If the frame is over 1.8m (6ft) wide, add further pegs to strengthen the sides.

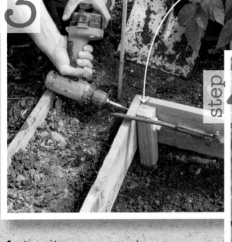

step 3

Hammer in the corner pegs and ensure the frame is level. Use screws to attach the frame to the pegs, holding it in position if necessary.

step 4

Carefully cut the landscape fabric using a sharp knife or scissors, leaving it slightly larger than the frame itself. Lay the fabric in the frame and tuck the edges in neatly around the sides.

4 In order to contain the ericaceous compost, and to prevent deep-rooted weeds, lay landscape fabric in the bottom of the bed.

5 Fill around the outside of the frame with the excavated soil. The top of the frame should be slightly proud of the soil to prevent lime leaching into it. The bed is now ready for filling.

step 5

Pour in the ericaceous compost, level it, then firm it down. The compost should come to about 2.5cm (1in) below the top of the frame to make watering easier.

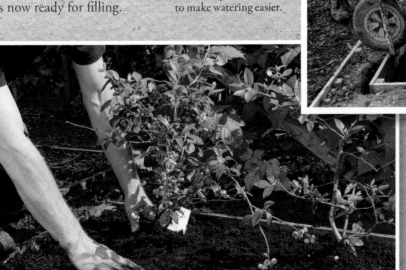

The soil must be kept moist, but not waterlogged, using rainwater and not tap water whenever possible. A water butt may need to be kept just for this reason.

Blackberries & Hybrids

These delicious fruits are so easy to grow that one of the difficulties is keeping the plants' growth in check. There are lots of hybrids to choose from, including tayberries, loganberries, tummelberries and the beautiful red-stemmed Japanese wineberries. Named varieties of blackberries are always sweeter and juicier than the wild forms found in hedgerows.

Netting As the berries start to ripen, place nets over the plants to prevent birds from stripping off all the berries.

Growing

Despite their vigour, blackberries require a sheltered site if they are to fruit well, although they will tolerate poorer soil than most fruits and can be grown in light shade. Hybrid berries prefer better-quality soil. Prior to planting, construct a training system to enable you to tie in their rampant growth. Such a system need consist of nothing more than parallel, horizontal wires fixed 35cm (14in) apart to a fence or between two stout posts.

◆ **CONTAINER-GROWN** blackberries and hybrid berries can be bought and planted all year round, but it is best to avoid extreme hot or cold weather. Bare-root canes are only available from late autum to late winter. These should be planted out immediately to prevent their roots from drying out.

Planting

Whether you have chosen to plant bare-root canes or container-grown plants (see right), prepare the soil by digging it over thoroughly to remove any weeds. You should also enrich the soil before planting by digging in plenty of well-rotted organic matter. After planting, prune the canes back to 20cm (8in) above soil level and water well. Keep the plants well watered throughout the summer months.

Make the hole Dig out a hole, using the pot to determine the size of hole needed. Make the hole slightly wider than the rootball.

Remove the plant Remove the blackberry from its pot and gently tease out the roots from the rootball.

Position the plant Place the plant so that it is level with the soil and fill the hole using a 50:50 mix of soil and garden compost.

loganberries

tayberries

Routine care

Fruit develops on canes that were produced during the previous year's growing season. The canes can either be trained on a system of posts and wires or simply grown against a fence or shed.

Tying in Tie in new canes during the summer. It is these canes that will produce fruit for the following year.

Growing tips

Harvesting Pick carefully to avoid squashing the delicate berries.

Most blackberries and hybrid berries are very thorny, so take care not to damage your eyes and wear gloves when handling them.

◆ **MULCH AROUND** the canes with plenty of well-rotted manure in early spring.

◆ **PRUNE THE CANES** between late autumn and early spring (see right).

◆ **TIGHTEN THE TRAINING WIRES** each year if they have become slack. Replace the posts if they have started to rot.

◆ **HARVEST THE BLACKBERRIES** when the fruit has turned black.

Pruning Untie the old canes just after they have finished fruiting and prune them right out.

Storing & Using

They can be made into: jams...pies... crumble...or can be frozen...

All these berries can be refrigerated for a few days and eaten fresh. You can freeze any glut (perhaps to serve as spiced fruit compote in winter) or turn it into jam. Alternatively, use the berries in a variety of desserts, some of which freeze well.

Blackberry & apple pie This traditional dessert has a sweet, tender crust and a melting, sweet-sharp filling. Make it and freeze for later use.

Freezing These berries all freeze very well. Freeze them on trays, then transfer them to freezer bags. They keep for up to 12 months.

blackberries

Gooseberries

If gooseberries conjure up an image in your mind of tart-tasting, hairy green fruit, then think again. Gooseberries now come in a wide range of varieties and colours and, when left to ripen properly, can be one of the sweetest and tastiest of fruits.

Planting Add plenty of organic matter to the soil. Plant bare-root bushes to the depth of the soil mark on the stem and container-grown plants so the compost is level with the soil.

'Hinnonmäki Red'

'Careless'

Growing

Gooseberries require a moist, heavy, fertile soil but will tolerate shade and can even be grown against a north-facing fence. They are usually grown as an open-centre bush on a small, 20cm- (8in-) high trunk. However, they can also be trained as vertical cordons 35cm (14in) apart and 1.5m (5ft) high or they can be fan-trained.

◆ **PRUNE BUSHES** twice a year. In winter you should prune them hard to reduce congested and crossing branches. In summer you should cut the new growth back to five leaves.

◆ **WATER GOOSEBERRIES** regularly during dry weather to avoid American gooseberry mildew (see p.234). Place a net over the bushes as they ripen to prevent birds from stripping all the fruit off the plants.

Harvesting Remove alternate, sharp-tasting fruits in early summer and use for cooking. Leave the remaining fruit to ripen and eat fresh in midsummer.

Storing & Using

Gooseberries can be used in: fools...jams...pies...
Currants can be used in: jellies...wines...sauces...

Keep gooseberries and currants in the fridge for a day or two, or freeze on trays and transfer to freezer bags, where they will keep for up to 12 months. Both fruits can be used to make a variety of delicious drinks and desserts, jams and jellies. They also make good accompaniments to savoury dishes.

Gooseberry fool
Add cooked berries to sugar and whipped cream for this dessert.

Currants

Packed full of vitamins, these berries come in a wide range of colours, from white through to pink, red and black. All are easy to grow, which makes them ideal for beginners.

whitecurrants

jostaberry

redcurrants

blackcurrants

Growing

Red, white, and pink currants are grown in exactly the same way as gooseberries (see opposite), so are suitable for growing as open-centre bushes or fans and cordons on north-facing walls.

◆ **BLACKCURRANTS** have a different growing habit (see below) and require a bright, sunny location in heavy fertile soil.

◆ **PRUNE BLACKCURRANTS** in winter, using loppers to remove about a third of the older wood at ground level.

◆ **BIRDS LOVE** all currants, so place netting over the ripening fruit, pulling it taut to prevent birds from getting entangled.

◆ **JOSTABERRIES** are a hybrid between a blackcurrant and a gooseberry, and produce large black, juicy berries. Resistant to American gooseberry mildew, plant them 2m (6ft) apart.

Planting

Blackcurrants are sold as "stools" – multi-stemmed bushes that send up new shoots from the base of the stool. Red, white and pink currant bushes grow from a "leg", or short stem. The different growing habits mean that the currants have different planting requirements (see right). Prior to planting, add plenty of organic matter to give the currants enough energy to enable them to produce lots of fresh new shoots.

Plant blackcurrants deep Blackcurrant stools are planted deeply to encourage new growth to shoot from below ground level.

Leave a "leg" Plant other currants so their "leg" is just above the surface of the soil. New growth emerges from the leg.

Water well Water plants in thoroughly, then mulch with well-rotted compost to retain water and suppress weeds.

fruit

trees & vines

apples • pears • plums, gages, & damsons • planting a fruit tree • cherries • peaches & nectarines • apricots • citrus & medlars • figs • quinces & mulberries • grapes & kiwis • melons

Planting

Apple trees can be planted all year round, but the best time is autumn. The soil is still warm then and the tree can get properly established before starting into growth in spring.

Prepare a hole After preparing the ground thoroughly, dig a hole that is double the circumference of the rootball.

Planting Plant containerized trees at the same depth as in their pots; bare-root trees to the soil marks on the trunks.

Apples

With over 800 varieties to choose from, there is an apple to suit everybody's taste. Not only do apples reward you with delicious fruit in the autumn, but they also provide a striking display of blossom in the spring. Apple trees can be grown in the smallest of spaces and are even suitable for growing in pots and containers.

Growing

Dessert apples require a warm, sheltered site so their fruit will ripen fully, although cooking apples will tolerate some shade. There are various methods of training fruit trees for small spaces but two of the most popular are oblique cordons and espaliers.

♦ **OBLIQUE CORDONS** are single stems or trunks planted at a 45-degree angle with short branches or spurs along their length.

♦ **ESPALIERS** have a series of parallel, horizontal branches that are trained flat against a fence.

♦ **CHECK THE ROOTSTOCK** when selecting an apple tree for a small space. Certain rootstocks will restrict the tree's growth so it won't outgrow your space. The most suitable rootstocks are M27, M9 and M26. Ask at your local garden centre for advice and details.

Support Trees need supporting with a post and tree-tie to keep them upright when young.

'Egremont Russet'   'Cox's Orange Pippin'   'McIntosh'   'Chivers Delight'   'Fiesta'

Pollination

Most apple trees require other apple trees fairly nearby to pollinate them. The trees should all flower at the same time so the bees can fly from the flowers on one tree to those on another. This ensures that the flowers will be pollinated and will set fruit.

Routine care

Cordons and espaliers should be pruned once a year in late summer by pruning back the new growth to one or two buds. Freestanding trees should be pruned in winter by removing crossing branches and dead wood. Keep the area around your apple trees free of weeds and water during dry periods.

◆ **THIN THE FRUITLETS OUT** in midsummer, reducing the clusters to one or two apples. This will ensure that those that remain will grow to full size.

◆ **HARVEST EARLY VARIETIES** in late summer, and late varieties in late winter.

Picking fruit
Harvest the fruit by gently cupping it in the hand and giving it a slight twist.

'Bramley'

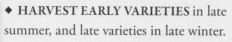

'Ribston Pippin'

Storing & Using

They can be used in: pies... puddings...chutneys... crumbles...or stored... or frozen...

Late apples store very well, either wrapped in waxed paper in crates or loose in sacks. Make sure the fruit is not damaged though or it will rot. Early varieties will only keep for a short time. If you have a glut of apples, you can stew them gently and freeze for use in winter to make pies or crumbles, or you can make apple juice and chutneys.

Store Late apples are the only ones worth storing. A cool shed or garage where humidity is low is the ideal place.

Chutney Apple chutney has a tangy, sweet flavour and goes very well with cheeses such as Cheddar, Cheshire or white Stilton. It also complements cold meats such as ham and meat pies.

Apple pie This is a traditional, comforting dish, often served with custard, cream or ice cream. The combination of sweet, flaky pastry and spiced fruit is unbeatable.

Pears

Pears have an unfair reputation for being tricky to grow, but in fact they are just as easy as apples. They have a delicious, soft buttery texture and a sweetness that is hard to beat. You can grow them in small spaces – some varieties are even suitable for containers – and their pure white springtime blossom is a lovely sight to behold.

Fertilizer

Pears are hungry plants and benefit from a general-purpose granular feed sprinkled around the roots in spring. Mulch afterwards with garden compost or manure.

Containers Pears make beautiful specimens in containers but will need watering daily during summer. Make sure the container is frost-resistant and re-pot into fresh compost every couple of years.

Growing

Pears require a warm, sheltered site with well-drained soil and full sun in order for their fruits to ripen fully. Because they flower early, they can be susceptible to spring frosts, so planting them in a sheltered site is especially important.

◆ **PEARS REQUIRE** a rich soil, so prepare it before planting by digging in plenty of organic matter. Plant trees that have a dwarf rootstock (usually Quince A or C) to restrict the size. They can be grown as cordons or espaliers (see p.208).

◆ **FLOWERS MUST** be pollinated before they can set fruit. If there are no pear trees nearby, you will need to plant at least two varieties that flower at the same time.

'Bartlett'   'Joséphine de Malines'   'Concorde'   'Doyenné de Comice'

Routine care

Cordons and espaliers should be pruned at the end of summer by reducing the new growth to one or two buds. Freestanding trees and trees grown in containers should be pruned when the tree is dormant in winter. Do this by thinning out any congested and crossing branches.

◆ **THIN EACH CLUSTER** of pears out in midsummer to prevent over-cropping and to allow the remaining fruits to ripen fully.

◆ **PROTECT SMALL** young trees by covering them with a layer of fleece whenever frosts are predicted.

Harvest Pears are ready to harvest from late summer to autumn. Pick them when they are slightly under-ripe and leave to ripen indoors.

Growing tips

Pears are relatively easy to grow and once planted should be easy to maintain. Keep the area around the trunk free of weeds and prune once a year.

Pear drop "June drop" is a natural process that allows the tree to shed excess fruitlets. Do not thin the pears until after this has occurred.

Watering Young trees need watering every few days during dry periods. They must not dry out when in flower or fruit.

Storing & Using

They can be used in: pies...puddings... salads...cakes...relishes...pickles...or stored...or frozen...

Pears can ripen rather suddenly, so once picked, keep an eye on them. Store later varieties in waxed paper, as apples (see p.209). They will keep for a few months. To freeze, choose ripe but not over-ripe specimens, peel and quarter, dip in water with a little lemon juice, then drain and poach in syrup. Freeze in the cooled syrup for up to 9 months.

Pear tart This makes an elegant dinner-party dessert. Pears also lend themselves to cakes and relishes, to being poached in wine and to being used raw in summer salads.

'Conference' 'Beth' 'Beurré Hardy' 'Kosui'

Plums, Gages, & Damsons

These soft, juicy fruits with their beautiful, translucent skin are the quintessence of summer. They are easy to grow, requiring minimal pruning, and they often provide bumper crops, which is extremely rewarding. Plums and their close relatives, the gages, are one of the sweetest and most delicious fruits when freshly picked from the tree, whereas damsons, which are smaller, make the best jam imaginable.

'Merryweather Damson'

Growing

Plums require a warm, sunny site with free-draining soil. Because their early-spring blossom can be susceptible to frosts, choose a sheltered site. They thrive in rich, fertile soil so add plenty of organic matter before planting.

◆ **PLUMS CAN BE FAN-TRAINED** against a fence or trellis or they can be grown as a freestanding tree. They are not suitable for growing as cordons or espaliers.

◆ **'PIXY' ROOTSTOCKS** are usually used for growing plums. These will restrict the overall size of the tree.

◆ **MOST PLUM VARIETIES**, such as 'Victoria', are self-fertile. That means you only need a single tree, which is ideal if you don't have much room.

Trees in pots Plums will thrive in a pot but ensure that is has adequate drainage and that it can be watered once a day during dry weather, especially in summer.

Thinning Fruitlets should be thinned out in early summer to 5–8cm (2–3in) apart. This allows the remaining fruit to ripen fully.

'Cambridge Gage'   'Czar'   greengage   'Victoria'   'Opal'

Planting

A healthy tree will reward you with fruit for at least 25 to 30 years, so it is worth preparing the soil well prior to planting. Thoroughly dig over the planting area, breaking up any pans (layers of dense soil, usually found just below the topsoil). Pans are largely impervious to water and so can restrict the trees' growth.

Prepare a hole Dig a hole and plant the tree at the same depth as it was in its pot.

Fill Backfill the hole with a 50:50 mix of the original soil and good garden compost.

Water Attach the tree to a stout stake using a tree tie and water it in thoroughly.

Routine care

These fruit trees should only be pruned during the growing season. Avoid pruning them in winter as this makes them susceptible to diseases such as silver leaf and bacterial canker. Generally, it is best to prune plum trees as little as possible. Aim just to remove diseased, damaged or crossing branches.

◆ **PROTECT THE BLOSSOM** on young trees by wrapping them up in fleece when springtime frosts are predicted, but remove the fleece during the day to allow pollinating insects access.

Harvesting Pick plums when they feel slightly soft to the touch. They ripen at different times on the same tree, so check the fruit regularly. Leave the stalk on the fruit when you pick it.

Storing & Using

They can be used in: jams... crumbles...pies...puddings... or frozen...

Plums, gages and damsons do not keep for long, so they should be eaten, preserved or frozen for later use. They develop their flavour best while on the tree, so pick them when they are ripe and ready to eat. They keep for a few days in the fridge or can be frozen on trays, then transferred to freezer bags. They will keep in the freezer for up to 6 months.

Chutney Plum chutney will keep for up to 6 months. These fruits also make delicious jams, while damsons are traditionally used to make damson "cheese" – a dense preserve.

Crumbles Plums, gages and damsons all make delicious crumbles. If you prefer tart flavours, use damsons.

'Santa Rosa'　　mirabelle　　'Marjorie's Seedling'

Project
Planting a fruit tree

Planting a fruit tree on the allotment will create interest and structure on the plot and, of course, provide you with delicious fruit. Before planting, check that the tree isn't going to cast too much shade on your own or your neighbours' plots. Ensure the tree you are buying won't get too big, and is a variety that you like.

Bare-root trees

These are available when the trees are dormant and have finished growing for the year, usually between mid-autumn and late winter. Plant bare-root trees immediately after buying them. If that isn't possible, plant them into large pots as a temporary measure.

MATERIALS & TOOLS

- fruit tree, compost
- spade, tree stake, tree tie, sledgehammer, galvanized nail

Hammer the stake in prior to planting to avoid damaging the roots later on.

step **1**

step **2**

Lay a spade across the hole to ensure the tree is planted to the same depth as it grew on the nursery. Look for the soil mark on the trunk.

Year-old trees These are referred to as "maidens". Those with branches are called "feathered maidens", those without are known as "maiden whips".

1 Dig a hole and ensure that the tree will be planted at the right depth, which is the same level as the soil mark on the stem.

2 Drive in a stout wooden stake to a depth of about 60cm (24in) into the soil to support the growing tree.

step 3

step 4

Add compost to the soil from the hole at a 50:50 mix before backfilling. Firm the soil around the tree by lightly treading it in.

Attach the tree to the stake with a tree tie. Use a galvanized nail to prevent the tie from slipping down the stake.

Check that the "graft union", a harmless bulge in the trunk, is above the level of the soil.

step 5

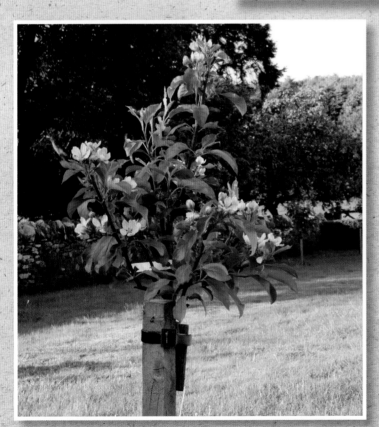

3 Replace the tree in the hole and fill it with soil. Make sure the soil settles fully around the roots, leaving no air pockets.

4 Firm down as you backfill the planting hole, but try not to compact the soil.

5 Support the tree, using a cushioned tree tie to prevent the tree rubbing on the stake.

Water well, then spread a mulch of well-rotted compost around the base of the tree.

Planting

Container-grown cherry trees can be planted at any time of year, but bare-root trees are only available from October to February and should be planted as soon after purchasing as possible.

Hole depth Plant containerized trees at the same depth as in their pots; bare-root trees to the soil marks on the trunks.

Fill Backfill the planting hole, and add compost and controlled-release fertilizer to the root area.

Stake Attach the tree to a stake using a tree tie. Water the plant well after planting to help it get established.

Cherries

A cherry tree dripping with luscious red fruit is not only a mouth-watering sight, but is a match for any ornamental plant in terms of beauty. And you do not need a huge plot to grow cherries; today, there are cherry trees for small plots, too. Enjoy sweet cherries fresh from the tree and use acid cherries for culinary purposes.

Growing

Sweet cherries require a warm site to ripen fully, whereas acid cherries will tolerate shady conditions and can even be fan-trained on north-facing fences. Cherry trees are no longer the preserve of orchards as recently developed rootstocks restrict size and vigour, making it possible to grow cherries in smaller spaces and gardens. They can be grown as freestanding trees on dwarfing rootstocks such as Colt or Gisela 5.

◆ **MOST MODERN** cherry varieties are self-fertile, meaning that you only need one tree. Others will need a second tree for pollination. Check the label before purchasing.

Fleece Protect the cherry blossom with fleece in spring if frost is predicted, to ensure a crop of cherries in the summer.

'Bing'

'Rainier'

Routine care

Prune both sweet and acid cherries when they are in leaf. Avoid pruning in winter or when it is raining as this can spread diseases such as silver leaf and bacterial canker. Prune sweet cherries minimally, only shortening over-long stems. Prune acid cherries by cutting a quarter of the branches that have fruited back to the next branch. Remove dead or damaged growth.

◆ **WATER YOUNG TREES** weekly during the summer months for the first couple of years. They will also benefit from an annual general-purpose granular feed in early spring, followed by a generous mulching with garden compost around the trunk.

◆ **WEED AROUND** the base of young trees to prevent the weeds competing for nutrients. Protect small trees from frosts during flowering by draping fleece over their branches.

◆ **USE SCISSORS OR SECATEURS** to harvest the cherries, leaving the stalks attached to the fruit.

Harvesting Hold the cherries while you harvest them to prevent the fruit dropping to the ground and spoiling.

'Morello'

Netting

Birds will quickly strip a tree of its sweet red fruits in a matter of hours. Place netting over small trees, using a system of canes or poles, with the netting draped over the top. Canes must be tall enough to clear the tops of the trees.

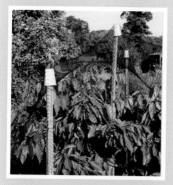

Peg down Secure the netting firmly along the ground with tent pegs to prevent birds sneaking underneath it.

Storing & Using

They can be used in: pies...jams... sauces...puddings...cakes...or preserve in brandy, vodka or rum... or stone and freeze...

The cherry season is relatively short so make the most of them while you can. They will keep in the fridge for up to a week in an open plastic bag but they also freeze very well and will keep in the freezer for up to 12 months. To freeze, remove the stones (see right), lay them out on a baking tray until they are frozen, then pack them in plastic bags and return to the freezer.

In brandy Cherries in brandy are a handy store cupboard treat, great for cooking, baking or simply spooned over ice cream.

Stoning Removing the stones of cherries before freezing them means you can easily use the thawed fruit in desserts and sauces without having to worry about the stones. There are plenty of cherry-stoning gadgets on the market these days that make the job relatively quick and easy.

Peaches & Nectarines

These two delicious fruits are basically the same and have the same growing requirements. Many modern varieties do not take up much space and, being self-fertile, you only need one tree. Both peaches and nectarines are easier to grow than you may think and should reward you with a good crop of luscious fruit.

Protection The delicate spring blossom needs protection from harsh frosts. If the blossom is destroyed, all chance of fruit is lost.

Pruning Peaches and nectarines fruit on growth produced the previous year, so prune in summer to remove the wood that has just produced fruit.

Growing

Peaches and nectarines require a warm, sunny site protected from harsh frosts and are usually grown as fans on south-facing walls or fences.

◆ **BUY ONE- OR TWO-YEAR-OLD** pot-grown trees from plant centres or online and check that they have been grafted onto dwarf rootstocks.

◆ **ALWAYS PRUNE** when the plant is in growth. Avoid pruning in winter as open wounds are susceptible to disease.

◆ **COVER THE PLANT** with waterproof sheeting during winter and early spring to protect it from peach leaf curl. Protect the flowers with fleece when frost is predicted.

'Lord Napier'

'Red Haven'

Thinning

Like most stone-fruits, peaches and nectarines need to be thinned out in summer, leaving the remaining fruit to ripen fully. If you fail to thin, the branches can snap from the weight. Also, overcropping in one year can result in no fruit at all the next.

First thinning When the fruits are the size of hazelnuts, thin to 10cm (4in) apart.

Second thinning Thin to a final spacing of 20cm (8in) when the fruits are walnut-sized.

Apricots

Closely related to peaches, apricots can be tricky to grow but the new, later-flowering apricots are less susceptible to spring frosts. Choose a dwarfing variety to save space on the allotment. Growing your own is well worth the effort; once you've tasted your own, shop-bought ones simply won't do.

Growing

Apricots grow best when trained as fans against south-facing walls and fences, although they will also ripen when grown as free-standing trees on very sheltered, favourable sites. Either way, they require a rich, heavy soil and full sun.

◆ **PLANT TREES** in spring or late autumn and keep them well-watered during their first year after planting.

◆ **FAN-TRAINED TREES** must be tied to a system of parallel rows of horizontal wires.

◆ **PROTECT THE BLOSSOM** with horticultural fleece when frosts are predicted.

Storing & Using

They can all be used in: sauces...purées... sorbets...tarts...cobblers...pies...compotes...

Peaches, nectarines and apricots are delicious eaten straight from the tree but they will keep in the fridge for a few days. They can also be frozen for up to 12 months. To freeze, remove the stones, poach the fruit lightly in a sugar solution, then cool and freeze in the liquid.

Preserving in brandy All stone-fruit can be preserved in alcohol and will keep for 12 months.

Making jam Peaches, nectarines and apricots all make delicious jam that will keep for 12 months. You must add pectin for the jam to set.

Wasp trap Hang wasp traps around the tree to prevent wasps from destroying your treasured crop of apricots.

apricot

Training & pruning

Apricots, like all members of the stone-fruit family, should be pruned when in full growth. If you prune them in winter, the open wounds make them susceptible to silver leaf (see p.236) and canker (see p.234).

Pinch out shoots In springtime, pinch out overcrowded young shoots to leave a space of about 10cm (4in) between each one.

Tie in shoots In midsummer, tie some of the young shoots to the support. These will provide the structure and fruit for the following year.

Trim new growth In late summer, use secateurs to cut some of the new growth back to about three leaves.

Citrus & Medlars

Citrus plants should be grown under cover in cooler climates but their benefits include attractive, evergreen foliage, scented flowers and fruit all year round. Medlar trees are fully hardy and provide a wonderful ornamental feature, with their beautiful blossom and quirky-looking fruits that are perfect for jam-making and jellies.

Medlars Looking like a cross between an apple and a rose hip, medlars must be nearly rotten before they can be eaten.

Medlar flowers Their pretty pink-tinged flowers make medlars worth growing for their ornamental qualities alone.

Growing

◆ **WHEN BUYING CITRUS** trees, look out for hardier varieties. Most require all-year-round protection in a polytunnel but Meyer lemons and kaffir limes are worth trying outside. Grow citrus trees in pots, then you can remove them from the polytunnel during warm spells. Wrap tender citrus plants in fleece during cold periods, even if you are growing them in a polytunnel. Prune the trees lightly to remove diseased or dead branches and harvest the fruit when it is soft and smells fragrant.

◆ **GROW MEDLARS** as small trees or bushes – choose varieties that have been grafted onto quince rootstocks to restrict their size – and dig in some well-rotted manure or compost before planting. Being self-fertile, you only need one specimen. Medlars prefer a warm, sheltered site but will tolerate some shade. Prune in winter as you would an apple, but keep the pruning to a minimum once the medlar is established. Mulch around young trees each spring and feed with a general-purpose fertilizer.

Storing & Using

They can be used for: curds ...preserves...pickles...jellies ...drinks...cakes...pies...

Citrus fruits will keep in the fridge for a few weeks but keep for longer on the tree. Medlars must "blet", or break down, until sweet. To do this, leave them on the tree or store them in sawdust in a cool, dark place.

Lemon curd Keep this sweet treat in the fridge and use within 2 weeks of making.

Pickled lemons Used in Middle-Eastern and Moroccan cooking, these can be refrigerated for up to 6 months.

lime

lemon

Figs

Despite their balmy Mediterranean image, figs are hardier than you may think and can survive cold temperatures. The difficulty is getting them to produce ripe fruit. In warmer climates they will produce two crops a year; in cooler countries, you can only expect one.

Growing

Restrict roots Plant in a slab-lined hole to restrict the tree's root system and stimulate fruit production.

Figs require a warm, sheltered site in full sun. They are usually grown as fans on south-facing fences or as standards in pots.

◆ **PRUNE IN SPRING** or late summer by cutting out some of the older wood and leaving the new shoots. You can prune fig trees back hard if they have become too big and straggly.

◆ **COVER WITH FLEECE** during winter if the tree is small enough. Pot-grown figs can be moved to sheltered spots such as porches or sheds if very cold weather is predicted.

◆ **HARVEST THE FIGS** when they are soft and start to droop.

Routine care

The trick to getting figs to produce fruit is to restrict their root system. Either grow them in pots or in 60cm (24in) planting holes lined with patio slabs. Plant them either in spring or autumn.

Remove fruit in autumn Unripe figs larger than the size of a pea should be removed in autumn as they won't survive through the winter.

Prune at the base Figs may produce suckers at the base of the trunk. These should be removed with secateurs as soon as they appear.

Autumn drop Don't panic if lots of figs fall from the tree in early autumn. This is the tree's way of ensuring that the remaining fruits mature.

Storing & Using

They can be used in: cakes...puddings...preserves... compotes...salads...

Ripe figs spoil quickly so eat them as soon as you pick them or keep for a day or two in the fridge. Fig jam is delicious and sometimes hard to find, so why not use your glut to make some? You can also freeze figs whole; they will keep for up to a year.

Dried Figs can be dried in a very cool oven. Once dried, put them in bags and freeze for 4 days to kill any bugs. Defrost, then use within a few weeks.

fig

Savoury Fresh figs work in savoury dishes as well as sweet. Try with Parma ham or blue cheese.

Quinces

One of the more unusual fruits to grow, quinces bear beautiful flowers in spring, followed by large, yellow, pear-shaped fruits that ripen in autumn. These are too hard to eat raw but are delicious when cooked. Quinces form a small- to medium-sized tree, and may take several years before cropping heavily.

Blossom Quince trees produce beautiful white- or pink-flushed flowers in mid-spring, providing a splash of colour on the plot.

Storing & Using

They can be used in: jellies... jams...preserves...cheeses... pies...puddings...

Quinces are a wonderfully aromatic fruit and store well. Place undamaged fruit on shallow trays and store in a cool, dry, and dark place. Ensure they are not touching. They will keep for up to 3 months. Quinces can only be eaten once cooked.

Quince cheese This is a kind of preserved quince purée, served with cold meats and cheeses. It keeps in the cupboard for up to a year.

Growing

Quinces prefer fertile, well-drained soil in a warm, sheltered site. Their early flowers can be damaged by frost, meaning no fruit, so don't plant them in frost pockets. The trees can reach a height of about 3.5m (12ft), so choose a site that gives them room to grow, and consider the shade they will cast. Quinces are self-fertile but fruit better with a second tree nearby.

◆ **WATER TREES** planted recently during any dry periods.
◆ **FRUITS DEVELOP** singly at the tips of the previous year's growth and should be left on the tree for as long as possible, picking them before the first autumn frosts arrive.
◆ **TO PRUNE** remove and thin out of some of the older wood to encourage new shoots that will fruit in their second year.

Feature Quinces can produce an abundant crop of fruit in autumn, creating an attractive feature for the corner of the allotment.

quince

Mulberries

These trees are grown for their delicious, sweet, raspberry-shaped berries, which are widely regarded as something of a luxury. Growing to 10m (30ft) tall, however, mulberries are only suitable for larger allotments, and can take up to eight years before fruiting.

mulberries

Growing

Mulberries like moist but well-drained soil in a warm, sunny, and sheltered site. They are self-fertile, so only one tree is required to produce a harvest. Plant trees in late autumn or early spring.

◆ **MULCH YOUNG** trees with well-rotted manure around their base. Give them a general-purpose granular feed each spring.

◆ **PRUNE LIGHTLY** as the wounds will bleed readily and don't heal quickly, leaving them prone to infection. If necessary, prune in winter, removing damaged or crossing branches.

◆ **HARVEST FRUIT** when fully ripe from late summer to early autumn. Handle the berries carefully, as they are easily damaged, and the juice can stain fingers and clothing.

Storing & Using

They can be used in: jellies... jams...preserves...tarts...or can be used to favour gin...

Mulberries are best eaten or cooked as soon as they are picked, although the berries will keep in the fridge for a few days. The soft fruit is not suitable for freezing as it turns to pulp when defrosted. Tarts and puddings made using mulberries freeze well.

Mulberry jam The berries can be used on their own to make jam, or mixed with other fruits, such as apples, strawberries, and raspberries, for a mix of flavours.

Wine Mixed with grape juice concentrate, then allowed to ferment and age, mulberry wine is a treat.

Black or white?

There are two types of mulberry commonly available, with either black or white fruits. Although both produce edible berries, black mulberries are far tastier, whereas white mulberries are best grown as an ornamental.

White mulberries These are grown for their decorative qualities, and have historically been used to feed silkworm caterpillars for silk making.

Black mulberries These are the ones to grow for their fruit, producing dark, juicy berries with an intense flavour that is hard to beat.

Grapes

If you have ever fancied producing your own wine, then having an allotment gives you the opportunity to try. Wine grapes are climbing plants and can be accommodated in small outdoor spaces as long as they have room to climb upwards. Dessert grapes are less hardy but if you are lucky enough to have a greenhouse, they are just as easy to grow.

'Black Hamburg'

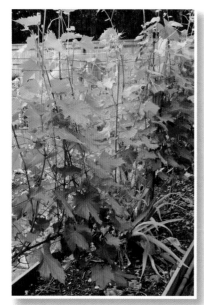

Growing on an allotment Grapes are easy to grow but you should give them a high-nitrogen fertilizer in winter and water newly planted vines in dry weather.

Growing

Wine grapes require a sunny, sheltered site to ripen fully. Fortunately, they aren't too fussy about soil type – after all, they grow in soils ranging from the shallow, flinty, chalk soils of Champagne in France to the rich, fertile soils of the Barossa valley in Australia.

◆ **CREATE A MINI-VINEYARD** on your plot by planting the grapevines 1m (3ft) apart in rows and with 1.5m (5ft) between each row. Plant the vines in early spring.

◆ **GRAPEVINES ARE CLIMBING PLANTS** so they need a system of horizontal parallel wires for their tendrils to cling to. They can also be trained up pergolas and arches or as a screen to create shade and privacy on the plot.

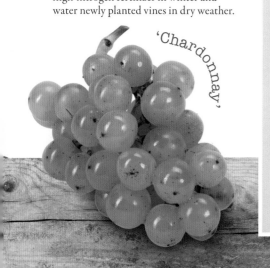
'Chardonnay'

Pruning

Grapevines are rampant growers and need a regular winter prune to keep their growth in check and maintain a neat and tidy appearance. You can also give them a light trim in summer – prune their new growth back to about five leaves.

First prune After planting, prune vines back to 30cm (12in) above soil level.

Mature prune With vertical cordons, prune the new growth back to two buds in winter.

Thinning

You don't need to thin individual wine grapes as they are small and form tight, close bunches that can easily be crushed for wine-making. However, dessert grapes do benefit from this rather laborious process as it helps the remaining fruit to develop to its full size and optimum sweetness. Thinning also protects the branches from splitting under the weight of the fruit.

Flowering Tiny buds appear prior to flowering. Keep the bunches dry at flowering time to promote fruit set.

Thinning Use a pair of scissors to thin out the grapes, starting off by removing the smallest grapes and any that are diseased.

Thinned After thinning, about one-third of the grapes should remain on each bunch, leaving space for them to develop.

Harvesting

Grapes require a long season to ripen. Although they may look translucent and feel soft, their sweetness may still not have developed fully. The best test for deciding when they are ready is to pick a few and taste them. If they taste sharp, leave them a little longer to ripen properly.

Kiwis

Another climbing fruit plant that is worth growing on the allotment is the kiwi. Do be warned, though – they make lots of luxuriant, rampant growth and will need a sturdy structure to scramble up. Most varieties require both a male and female plant to produce fruit, although modern varieties, such as 'Jenny', are self-fertile. New plants fruit after three or four years.

Harvest Kiwis ripen late in the year and should be harvested before the first frosts. They will continue to ripen indoors in the fruit bowl.

Storing & Using

They can be made into: wines...jellies... puddings...salads...

Grapes are best eaten soon after harvesting, though you can keep them in the fridge for a few days. They can even be frozen and make a tasty treat straight from the freezer. Use defrosted grapes in jams and jellies, as the fruit goes mushy when defrosted.

Crushing To make wine, first you need to crush or mash the grapes well with a potato masher.

Homemade wine Making your own wine is an easy and satisfying process; you don't need to buy a lot of specialized equipment.

Grape jelly Grapes are a good choice for making jellies, which are a change from jams.

kiwi

Melons

Possibly the most delicious of all fruits, this sweet, juicy, tender, climbing annual requires a very warm sunny site to ripen fully outdoors. Alternatively, they can be grown in polytunnels, cloches, and greenhouses, which allow a wider range of varieties to be tried. Types include honeydew with firm yellow flesh, cantaloupe with orange-coloured flesh, and musk which has green-netted skin.

Melon collar If you fit a collar around the stem, you can water the surrounding soil without wetting the plant, which reduces the risk of diseases.

Pollination Melons produce both male and female flowers. Female flowers have a swelling just below the base. To help with pollination, male flowers can be picked and pushed into the female ones so that the pollen transfers across.

Growing

Melons can be bought as young plants or can be easily raised from seed in spring. If growing outdoors, dig over the soil and add plenty of bulky, well-rotted organic matter, such as manure or garden compost.

◆ **HARDEN OFF** plants in a cold frame or porch for a few days before planting outside once the risk of frost has passed. Plant melons 60cm (24in) apart.

◆ **ALTERNATIVELY**, they can also be planted in growing bags with no more than two per bag, or in 30cm (12in) containers.

Sowing seeds

Melons are grown from seed started indoors, as sowing outdoors is too unreliable. Plants intended for growing under cover in a greenhouse or polytunnel should be sown in early spring. Plants for outdoors are sown in mid- to late spring. When selecting varieties, read the back of the seed packet carefully to avoid disappointment, as some types won't ripen outdoors. Melons are large plants so don't sow more than you have space for.

Sowing Fill small pots with general-purpose or seed compost, lightly firm it down, and water before sowing four seeds per pot. Cover the seeds with compost.

Mini-cloche Secure a clear plastic bag over each pot to help retain moisture. Stand the pots in a warm greenhouse or on a bright windowsill indoors.

Growing on When they have germinated, grow the seedlings on under cover for a few weeks to develop. Thin the seedlings or pot them on as required.

Planting outside

Melons are hungry, fast-growing plants, and require rich, moisture-retentive soil to crop well. They also need sturdy supports for their climbing stems, or enough space if allowed to trail across the soil. Melons grow well in containers and growing bags, which can be positioned to provide the best spot, although they will require plenty of water.

Prepare the soil The soil should be thoroughly dug over before planting, digging in plenty of well-rotted organic matter.

Lay plastic To help warm the soil, retain moisture, and control weeds, plant outdoor melons through black plastic.

Clean fruit Planting through plastic prevents the fruits of trailing plants from sitting on the soil, keeping them clean.

Routine care

Melons can be left to scramble along the ground but they take up less space when trained vertically, which also keeps the fruits away from many pests. Provide support using canes and string, and tie in the stems as they grow.

◆ **THIN FRUITS** out when they have reached the size of golf balls to leave about four per plant. Keep them watered and fed.

◆ **FRUITS TRAILING** on the ground should be placed on straw or wood to prevent them rotting on the damp soil.

◆ **CROP MELONS** when they develop a sweet scent in summer.

'Galia'

'Ogen'

Support When growing melons vertically, the fruits also need to be supported to prevent damaging the stems. Attach strings or pieces of netting to form a sling when the fruits reach about the size of a cricket ball.

Storing & Using

They can be used in: salads...sorbets...smoothies...or can be eaten fresh...

Ripe melons should be stored in the fridge, where they will keep uncut for up to 5 days. Once cut, they should keep for 3 days, but should be wrapped to prevent the flesh becoming dry. Melons can also be sliced or their flesh scooped out into balls, and frozen. The best way to enjoy melon is simply sliced.

HELP
Troubleshooting guide

Dealing with problems

If you are new to gardening, problems such as pests, diseases, deficiencies, and bolting can sound a bit daunting, so it is best to be well informed as there are often steps you can take to keep your crops safe. Monitoring crops closely will help combat any problems that arise and keeping them in a good, healthy condition will help to prevent them taking hold.

Keeping plants in good health

Remember that prevention is better than cure – keeping plants healthy should help them to fend off many common problems.

◆ **KEEP PLANTS WEED-FREE** so that they are not competing for nutrients. Hoe between rows regularly to get rid of annual weeds and dig out perennials carefully, removing all the roots.

◆ **WATER PLANTS REGULARLY** during the growing season and feed them with fertilizers to keep them strong and healthy. This will make them less prone to bolting, see right. Mulch around plants to retain moisture and suppress weeds.

◆ **PRUNE TREES AND SHRUBS** to remove diseased material and to increase air circulation in the canopy. Remove and destroy rotted or infected leaves or fruit as soon as they appear.

Bolting Some plants, such as spinach and lettuce, are susceptible to bolting – premature flowering that spoils the crop – if sown too early or not watered enough.

Overwatering The roots of crops may rot if they are not allowed to dry out, and this can also cause the fruit to split, especially if the plant is watered irregularly.

Underwatering If you don't water plants regularly enough in the growing season they will quickly wilt and die. Some plants need daily watering in hot, dry weather.

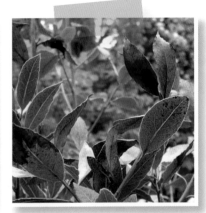

Frost damage Frost can damage flower buds and shrivel leaves and young shoots, turning them brown. If frosts threaten, protect crops with a fleece or cloche.

Natural methods

Nature has its own methods of providing defence but, as a gardener, you can always give your plants a helping hand. Planting wildflowers will attract insects such as ladybirds and lacewings, which will keep down the aphid population; it also encourages hedgehogs, which will help control slugs and snails. Erecting barriers is a simple but effective method of preventing pests from attacking your crops. Bespoke fruit cages to prevent bird damage can be purchased, but makeshift ones can be made simply with bamboo canes and a net. Some pests can be confused by planting other crops nearby. For example, the smell of onions confuses carrot fly, reducing the chances of infestation in both parsnips and carrots.

Beneficial wildlife Encourage helpful creatures into the garden by avoiding chemicals where possible, and create inviting habitats using wildflowers and piles of rotting logs.

Insect-proof netting Place fine, insect-proof meshes over plants that are susceptible to damage from butterflies and moths and their larvae, such as cabbages and carrots.

Companion planting Plant flowers near your crops to lure away pests. Marigolds, for example, keep whitefly off tomatoes, and onions can keep carrot fly away from carrots.

Pests, diseases, and deficiencies

◆ **SOIL PROBLEMS:** If your plant is looking sickly it is possible that the soil is unsuitable. Check the pH level with a kit (see p.21) to see whether conditions are too alkaline or acidic. Alternatively, check the soil isn't too heavy or light, preventing plants from growing properly. Water and feed plants in sandy soil regularly and improve the soil with organic matter. Plants in clay soil could get waterlogged, so dig in plenty of horticultural grit before planting.

◆ **DISEASES:** There are a range of diseases that can affect plants. Look closely to see if there are signs of mould or rotting, and act quickly to remove affected material from your site.

◆ **PESTS:** Larger pests such as birds and rabbits cause obvious damage, but check leaves and young shoots regularly to see if tiny insects are eating your crops. Use barriers to prevent them from infesting your crops to prevent problems later on.

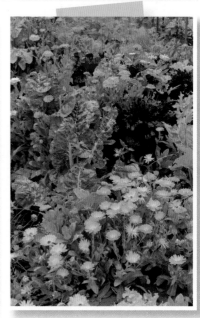

Disguising crops Camouflage your crops in amongst flowering plants. Not only will this look attractive, but it may help to keep pests at bay.

Gallery of pests

Very few crops are trouble-free, so you'll need to be vigilant and keep a close eye on your developing fruit and vegetables. Be proactive and take simple precautions when plants are young: place a net over trees to prevent bird damage or cover seedlings with horticultural fleece or cloches as a barrier to moths and butterflies. If pests do attack, use this gallery to identify them and follow the advice so that you can limit the damage and prevent pests devouring them.

Wasps These stinging pests go after the sugary flesh on most fruit crops. Hang up wasp traps on trees or place rotting fruit away from the fruit trees to lure them away.

Codling moth The larvae of this pest tunnel into apples and eat their way to the core. Hang pheromone traps in the trees or use an appropriate insecticide.

Carrot fly The larvae tunnel into carrots and parsnips, damaging the roots. Surround crops with 60cm (24in) high horticultural fleece and choose resistant varieties.

Leek moth These caterpillars bore into leeks and onions causing them to rot and die. Cover the crops with fleece to prevent the adult moth from landing on them.

Whitefly These suck the sap from leaves and excrete honeydew. Control includes using an appropriate insecticide or a parasitic wasp called *Encarsia formosa*.

Pea moth Adults lay their eggs on pea flowers in midsummer. They hatch, live inside the pod and eat the peas. Net summer crops to prevent the moth landing.

Asparagus beetle Both adults and larvae attack foliage and stems of asparagus plants causing loss of leaves and the stems to die back. Pick off beetles and dispose of them.

Vine weevils The adults eat notches out of the foliage but the larvae cause most harm by eating the roots, especially on potted crops. Use nematodes as biological control.

Aphids These sap suckers attack and destroy growing shoots and foliage. Rub them off with soapy water, crush them or use an appropriate insecticide.

Red spider mite These cause a bronzed, mottled effect on foliage, particularly inside greenhouses. Use biological controls or a fatty acid to control them.

Birds Fruit crops such as figs and cherries can be damaged or completely stripped by birds, which also decimate cabbages and other veg. Protect crops using netting.

Slugs These slimy pests attack and devour the stems and foliage of plants, particularly seedlings. Use biological controls, beer traps, or physical barriers to protect crops.

Black bean aphids These sap-sucking aphids attack broad beans causing distorted stems and foliage. Control by pinching out the top 8cm (3in) of the plant.

Plum leaf-curling aphids These insects cause severe leaf distortion on plum trees in spring. Use a plant oil winter wash to control eggs or an appropriate insecticide.

Caterpillars There are many different types of caterpillars and they mainly feed on leaves and stems. Remove by hand or net crops to prevent adults landing.

Apple sawfly The larvae damage fruitlets in late spring, causing affected fruits to drop off in summer or scarring larger apples. Remove and destroy infected fruit.

Gallery of diseases

No garden will escape disease completely, so it is important to learn to diagnose the many different types and how to deal with them. Many of them can be avoided by ensuring there is plenty of air circulation around the plants, keeping the roots moist, and removing and burning any infected material immediately. It is equally important to keep garden tools, pots, and seed trays clean. There are a limited number of fungicides available, so try to prevent fungi, viruses, and bacteria from occurring by practising good garden hygiene.

American gooseberry mildew The fruit becomes covered with a whitish fungus. Keep roots moist and choose resistant varieties such as 'Invicta' and 'Rokula'.

Tomato blight This fungus spreads rapidly and causes fruits to rot and brown patches to appear on stems and leaves. Remove the foliage and destroy.

Downy mildew This disease appears in warm, humid conditions causing brown patches on the leaves and whitish fungus underneath. Destroy infected material.

Cucumber mosaic virus This virus attacks cucumbers and other veg causing leaves to appear mottled and stunting growth. Destroy plants and wash tools afterwards.

Botrytis Grey mould is often worse in warm, humid weather. Fruit becomes covered in mould and rots. Increase air circulation and destroy infected material.

Canker This causes growths and distortion in existing wounds on tree trunks, eventually resulting in death. Remove infected wood and disinfect tools used.

Common potato scab A disease that causes raised brown markings on potato skins. Avoid dry or alkaline soils, lime before planting, and grow resistant varieties.

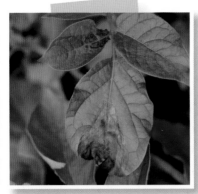

Chocolate spot This causes brown, chocolate-coloured spots on the foliage and pods of broad beans. Remove infected plant material and destroy immediately.

Onion white rot The symptoms are white, rotting bulbs and it can remain in the soil for many years. Practise crop rotation or grow in fresh soil in raised beds.

Potato blight The foliage and stems become brown and eventually wither and die. Remove stems immediately to prevent the infection destroying the crop beneath.

Clubroot This soil-borne disease distorts the roots of the cabbage family, causing foliage to flop over. Increase the pH by adding lime and improve the drainage.

Blossom end rot This mainly affects tomatoes and peppers, causing the ends of the fruits to rot. It is the result of calcium deficiency, so keep plants well watered.

Sclerotinia A fungal disease on lettuce, celery, beans, and other veg. The plants wilt, turn yellow, and fungus appears on the surface. Destroy plants immediately.

Damping off A fungal problem causing young seedlings in the greenhouse to collapse. Increase the air circulation and use clean pots and trays and mains water.

Rust This affects many plants, causing orange markings or pustules to appear on foliage and stems. Crop rotation helps but infected plants should be removed at once.

Brown rot This fungus affects fruit trees causing the fruit to turn brown and rot. Remove infected crops immediately and increase the air circulation in the canopy.

Honey fungus This attacks fruit trees. Roots develop white fungus and honey-coloured toadstools may appear. Remove affected plants and replace the soil.

Powdery mildew A whitish coating appears on leaves and shoots, affecting many fruit and vegetable crops. Try resistant varieties and water regularly.

Silver leaf This attacks plum, cherry, peach, and apricot trees, causing leaves to turn silver and branches to die back. Summer pruning reduces risk of infection.

Bitter pit Brownish indentations appear on apple skins and the flesh tastes bitter. Keep plants watered and mulched as it is caused by drought-induced calcium deficiency.

Raspberrry cane blight This disease causes the canes to become brittle and break easily, and the foliage withers. Prune to increase air circulation.

Peach leaf curl This affects peaches and nectarines, causing leaves to turn reddish and blister, curl up, and drop off. Keep buds dry in winter with rain covers.

Shothole Brown markings appear on the leaves of cherries or plums, which drop out leaving holes. It can be caused by bacterial canker or powdery mildew.

Scab Brown angular markings appear on the leaves and fruit of apples and pears. Remove infected leaves and fruit on heavy infestations and rake up leaves in autumn.

Scorch Caused by overexposure to the sun or wind, the leaves turn brown and become brittle. Avoid watering at midday and protect greenhouse crops with shade.

Gallery of deficiencies

If your soil is lacking in essential nutrients, plants can become stunted or withered. Although deficiencies can have serious effects on crops, the problem can often be easily remedied by giving plants the missing nutrients.

Nutrients for healthy crops

Plants need a well-balanced diet for healthy growth, but if they are lacking in certain nutrients they will become sickly. At first glance, it may look like a pest or disease problem is affecting your crops. However, if there is no sign of fungus or insect damage, the problem could be due to deficiencies in the soil. A simple fertilizer application is usually all that is required to resolve the situation.

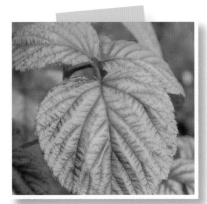

Iron Lack of iron causes leaves to turn yellow between the veins. The edges often turn brown, too. Apply chelated iron to the soil and mulch with acidic material.

Magnesium This is a common deficiency: the leaves turn yellow and darker patches appear between the veins. Spray diluted epsom salts over the foliage.

Potassium Affected plants have brown crispy leaves and the flowers often do not set fruit. Apply a liquid feed high in potash, such as a tomato feed.

Nitrogen The foliage turns yellow and the plant stops producing new green shoots. A general-purpose fertilizer and mulch should be applied to remedy the problem.

Boron This can cause a range of crops to split, particularly sweetcorn, and causes poor root development on root crops. Add borax to the soil or use a foliar feed.

Calcium Lack of calcium can cause blossom end rot or bitter pit, as it affects the plant's uptake of water. Apply lime to the soil and keep plants regularly watered.

Gallery of weeds

A weed is defined as any plant growing where it is not wanted, and on an allotment you must be careful not to allow weeds to spread to other plots. Digging or hoeing them off manually is often a good way to tackle them, but if you don't grow organically, it is sometimes necessary to use weed killer. As with pests and diseases, prevention is better than cure.

Goosegrass This sticky, clinging weed spreads rapidly through the veg plot but can easily be removed by pulling it out by hand.

Common problems

Weeds should be removed from around crops because otherwise they will compete for nutrients and water, and they can shade and smother the fruit and vegetables. They also harbour pests.

◆ **PREVENTION:** Cover up bare soil as quickly as possible with weed-suppressing membrane; otherwise weeds will spread to it. If the soil is going to be bare for a while, consider sowing a green manure that will increase the soil fertility and smother any weeds.

◆ **WEED KILLERS:** If you're happy to use chemicals, weed killers can be ideal for tackling perennial weeds, such as dock and bindweed. Choose a "systemic" treatment, which is absorbed by the weed and will kill the roots. Avoid spraying other nearby plants.

◆ **FLAME GUNS:** These can be used to burn off the foliage, but they will not kill perennial roots.

◆ **DIGGING:** The most effective method of removing all weeds is to dig them out, root and all.

◆ **HOEING:** This is an effective method of removing annual weeds.

◆ **MULCHING:** Use compost or manure to suppress weeds and stop them emerging.

Hairy bittercress This small, low-growing annual is a prolific spreader if it produces seed. Hoe it off before it flowers.

Weed-proof fabric Landscape fabric can be placed around trees and covered with mulch to prevent weeds.

Dandelion A familiar site on allotments and lawns, it has a deep taproot which must be dug up to prevent its regrowth.

Annual meadow grass This annual grass can rapidly spread and seed all over the allotment if not hoed off before it sets seed.

Creeping thistle This perennial thistle is prickly and difficult to get rid of. Either dig it out or use a weed killer.

Shepherd's purse This annual weed produces purple, heart-shaped pods and should be dug up before it sets seed.

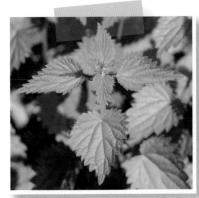

Stinging nettle A very common weed that needs digging out thoroughly to remove all the roots, or use a weed killer.

Groundsel This annual produces white seedheads and daisy-like flowers. Either hoe or dig it up before it spreads.

Dock This deep-rooted perennial, with its large leaves, should be dug out completely. Remove all the roots or use a weed killer.

Ragwort This invasive perennial can quickly take over the plot if not kept under control. Dig it out with a fork.

Creeping buttercup Preferring damp soil, this perennial is a persistent weed so the entire root system should be dug out.

Bindweed This climbing perennial is very difficult to eradicate. Consider using weed killer in severe cases.

Pruning

All fruit trees and bushes need pruning if they are to crop well and remain healthy. Although this process can look daunting, there are just a few basic techniques to master. All that is needed is a good pair of secateurs, a pruning saw, some loppers, and a bit of confidence to get you started.

Why prune at all?

Most fruiting trees and shrubs crop on newer growth, usually between one to three years old. Pruning encourages them to produce strong new stems that will then bear fruit. Pruning trees also removes congested growth in the canopy that would block sunlight reaching the developing fruit and ripening them. It is also essential for removing dead, damaged, or diseased wood from trees and bushes. If left unpruned, trees and bushes become weaker, producing small, poor-quality crops, and are more prone to diseases. Pruning also keeps plants tidy and at a manageable size, preventing them from encroaching on paths or casting excess shade.

Remove weak growth Thin spindly stems are unlikely to produce fruit, and just congest the tree canopy, blocking out sunlight and reducing airflow. They should be removed every year.

Tool maintenance

Pruning tools need to be kept sharp and oiled to maintain their performance. Blunt saws and secateurs can rip plant growth, leave jagged edges, or cause unnecessary wounds. These can become infected by diseases that can spread throughout the plant, possibly even killing it. Pruning tools should always be cleaned after use, especially when pruning out diseased growth, to prevent spreading it to other plants pruned later.

Oiling a saw Before putting saws away after pruning, brush away any sawdust on the blade and wipe it with an oily rag.

Remove rust If rust spots appear on secateurs or other tools, remove them using wire wool and a drop of oil.

General pruning tips

Using the correct pruning tool is essential to give clean cuts, and to make the task easier. Secateurs are ideal for pruning stems that are no larger than the circumference of a thick pencil. For thicker stems, use a pruning saw. These have long, thin blades that cut cleanly, and are designed to get into tight canopies, and cut at difficult angles. Long-handled loppers are also useful for pruning larger branches, although they can cause crush damage unless they are kept sharp. However, they are perfect for cutting up all the prunings into small pieces. Telescopic loppers are useful for reaching branches higher up.

Branches Use a pruning saw to cut larger branches and get close to the trunk.

Diseased stems Sterilize tools after pruning diseased growth.

New shoots Wispy, new growth can be removed as it will not produce fruit.

Good cut This is a perfect cut, not too close to the growing bud.

Bad cut This rip was caused by blunt secateurs that did not cut cleanly.

How to prune fruit trees

Pruning cuts should be made just above a bud. Avoid leaving stubs, as these eventually die back causing infection. However, don't cut right next to the bud either, as this can also cause damage. To make a clean cut with secateurs, the sharp, thinner blade should be facing the branch to be retained, and the thicker beak should face the side of the branch to be removed (see above). This avoids crushing the end of the remaining branch. Ideally, the cut should be angled slightly away from the bud. When removing large branches, remove the majority of the weight first to prevent tearing the bark when it is finally removed. Don't make the final cut flush with the trunk, as this can cause dieback. Instead, leave a small protrusion or "collar", which will eventually callous over, preventing any infection getting in. Try to keep the tree as balanced as possible, ensuring one side is not higher than the other. Remove upright vigorous shoots, and any that cross or rub.

When to prune fruit trees

Fruit trees should be pruned at specific times of year, either to encourage new growth shortly afterwards or to reduce the risk of infection. Trees may also be pruned lightly in summer to remove excess growth or wayward stems.

- Apple and pear trees should be pruned in winter while they are dormant.
- Trees trained as espaliers, cordons, and stepovers (see p.242) should be pruned in late summer.
- Plums, peaches, nectarines, and cherries are pruned in late spring or early summer to avoid silver leaf disease.

Trained fruit trees

Most fruit trees can be trained and pruned over several years into attractive shapes, such as knee-high stepovers, single-stemmed cordons, and elegant fans and espaliers. The purpose of this is usually to save space, and to allow more crops or varieties to be squeezed onto the plot. It can also be to make best use of a warm, south-facing aspect or wall, training the tree to face the sun. Conversely, it can be to reduce the shade cast by the tree, allowing other crops to flourish. Fruit trees can also be trained purely for ornamental reasons, and can create a beautiful and fruitful feature on the allotment.

Oblique pear cordons Grown as a single stem with short branches, the trunks of apple and pear trees can be trained at an angle.

Stepovers Apple stepovers need to be grafted onto extremely dwarfing rootstocks. They are ideal for edging vegetable plots.

Fans Cherries, nectarines, and peaches are often grown as fans, usually against a warm wall. Other fruit trees can also be trained in this way and will crop freely.

Espaliers This type of training probably produces the prettiest shape of tree you can grow. Once established, new growth simply needs pruning back to one or two leaves in late summer to keep the plant compact and to retain its shape. Apples and pears are the most suitable fruit trees for espaliers.

Pruning fruit bushes

Fruit bushes and canes should be pruned each year to encourage strong, fruiting growth and to remove any dead, diseased, or damaged stems. Some, like gooseberries, have sharp thorns, so wear gloves as a precaution. Most should be pruned to create a bright, airy, open centre.

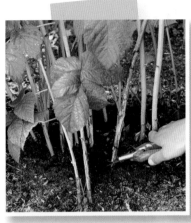

Summer raspberries Prune summer-fruiting raspberries after they have cropped. Cut out the old canes at the base and tie in new ones.

How to prune

Gooseberries and red- and whitecurrants are pruned in summer and winter to produce fruiting buds at the base of new stems, which will then crop the following year. Blackcurrants are pruned at the same time as picking by cutting stems that have fruited back to the base. To prune blueberries, remove the lower side branches and cut about one-third of the oldest stems to the base in spring.

When to prune

Specific soft fruit plants have certain times in the year when they benefit the most from being pruned. Plants such as grapevines, redcurrants, and gooseberries can be pruned twice in the year.

- Grapevines, redcurrants, gooseberries, blackcurrants, blackberries: main prune in winter.
- Grapevines, gooseberries, redcurrants: prune in summer, cutting new growth back to five leaves.
- Autumn raspberries: winter.
- Summer raspberries: late summer.

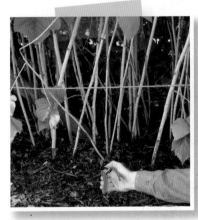

Autumn raspberries Prune all stems to the base in winter. Alternatively, cut some canes down by half, which will fruit slightly earlier.

Blackcurrants These are pruned in winter by removing a third of the oldest growth at the base of the plant. Use loppers or a pruning saw.

Blueberries Prune these like blackberries, removing about a third of the older wood and retaining younger material.

Redcurrants These plants also benefit from an extra summer prune, cutting new shoots back to five leaves. Use secateurs for this task.

Propagating plants

Most crops can be grown from seed, and although this is ideal for annual vegetables it is too slow for raising fruit bushes or perennial plants. Instead, to increase your stocks, take cuttings or suckers, or divide existing clumps.

Blueberries These shrubs can be propagated by taking 20cm (8in) long hardwood cuttings in winter and placing them into a pot filled with ericaceous compost. Take more than one cutting to increase your chances of success.

Fruit cuttings and suckers

Many fruit bushes can be propagated by taking hardwood cuttings in winter. In a sheltered section of the allotment, improve a small patch of soil with sharp grit – unless it is already free-draining. Cut 20cm (8in) long, healthy, young stems from the fruit bush, and push the bottom two thirds of each into the gritty soil. Water them during any dry spells, and by next spring they should have rooted, ready to plant out. This technique can be used for redcurrants, blackcurrants, and gooseberries.

Suckers These are vigorous new shoots that appear from the base of certain plants. They root and grow quickly if potted up and watered well.

◆ **BLACKBERRIES** and raspberries produce suckers at the base. These can simply be dug up in spring and grown on in pots, until planted out.

Lifting and dividing perennial crops

Once planted, perennial crops stay in the soil for several years, gradually forming large clumps. Over time, these clumps can become congested and the plant becomes weak. The best way to revive them is to lift the whole plant in spring or autumn and split it into sections, replanting only the strongest parts. This often produces lots of healthy new plants, more than you may need, so consider giving any surplus ones away.

Herbs Many perennial herbs spread, either creeping across the soil or spreading via underground roots. This makes them easy to lift and divide in spring. Plant the new pieces back into the soil or grow them on in pots.

Strawberry runners

Strawberries are one of the easiest plants to propagate, as all the work has been done for you. They naturally produce "runners", which are mini plants on long stems. These can be pegged down, where they will take root in just a few weeks.

Peg down While the runner is still attached to the parent plant, peg it down into a pot filled with compost.

Cut free When the runner has produced several healthy new leaves, it can be severed from the main plant.

Don't be tempted

Sometimes there may seem an obvious way to grow your own plants for free but there can be good reasons not to do so.

◆ **FRUIT TREES** can be grown from pips but the resulting trees are unlikely to fruit well, if at all. Buy fruit trees instead.

◆ **POTATO TUBERS** will grow if planted but risk spreading diseases. Buy certified disease-free seed potatoes each spring.

◆ **SUPERMARKET GARLIC** is usually a different variety to what is grown in this country, and is unlikely to produce a good crop.

Fruit pips Easy and fun to raise from pips, fruit trees raised this way will usually disappoint, taking years to even reach flowering size.

Rhubarb This can form a large woody clump in time, which should be divided. Discard the centre and split the remainder into new plants with two healthy shoots each.

Asparagus Although this crop takes a long time to establish, mature plants can be lifted and split in autumn. Divide clumps into three or four healthy sections.

Globe artichoke These plants can be lifted in winter to reveal small plants called "offsets" at the base. Cut these off, pot them up, and grow them on.

Jerusalem artichoke This large plant is grown for its underground tubers, which, unlike potatoes, can be replanted to grow and crop the following year.

Glossary

Acid (of soil) With a pH value of less than 7, and suitable for acid-loving plants. (See pH).

Alkaline (of soil) With a pH value of more than 7, and suitable for lime-loving plants. (See pH).

Annual A plant that completes its life cycle of germinating, flowering, going to seed, and dying in one growing season. (See Perennial).

Backfill To refill the hole dug when planting a new plant, using soil or compost.

Bare-root Of plants sold with their roots bare of soil and not in pots.

Beer trap A method of trapping slugs whereby a container is plunged into the soil and filled with beer; the slug, attracted by the beer, falls in and can't get out.

Blanch 1) To exclude light from developing leaves or stems to make them tender, sweeter-tasting, and pale in colour. This is done by pulling soil up around the base of the plants or by placing a container over them. 2) To plunge vegetables into boiling water for a few minutes, before cooling quickly in iced water, drying, and freezing them in bags. This helps to retain the colour, flavour, and texture.

Blet To allow medlar fruits to over-ripen in order to make them palatable. They are picked from the tree and left in a dark, cool place to soften for several weeks.

Bolt To flower and run to seed prematurely at the expense of leaf or root production. This can sometimes happen to plants because of a change in daylight hours, a sudden cold spell, or a lack of water. Lettuce and spinach crops are prone to bolting.

Brassica A plant in the cabbage family, including swedes.

Brassica collar Circular pieces of cardboard, felt, or other material placed around the bases of brassica plants to prevent female cabbage root flies laying eggs in the soil surface, near their roots.

Catch crops The growing of quick-maturing crops in the interval between harvesting one main crop and sowing or planting another to make best use of space.

Chitting To place seed potatoes in a light, airy place, such as on a window ledge, prior to planting, to encourage the tubers to produce small growing shoots, called chits.

Cloche A temporary structure made from polythene or glass used to warm the soil before planting, encourage early growth, or to protect crops against frost damage.

Countersunk screw A screw which is inserted to sit flush with, or just below, the surface of the surrounding material.

Crop rotation A system by which crops are grown in different areas of a vegetable plot each year, in a three- or four-year cycle. It is used to help prevent the build-up of soil-borne pests and diseases that could otherwise occur.

Cure 1) To leave vegetables, such as pumpkins and squashes, outside in the sun after harvesting to allow their skins to harden, so they will store for longer. 2) To allow concrete to dry out slowly so it sets and hardens without cracking.

Cut-and-come-again A range of leafy salads and vegetables that can be harvested while young, then left to regrow, to harvest again a few weeks later.

Dibber A pointed hand tool, usually wooden, used to create holes in the soil in which to sow seeds or plant bulbs and sets.

Double digging A method of soil cultivation in which the soil is worked to a depth of two "spits", or double the depth of a spade to create a deep and healthy soil for plants to grow in.

Drill A shallow, straight trench made in the soil using a hoe or rake, in which to sow seeds. The soil is pushed back over the seeds after sowing.

Earthing up Drawing soil around the base of a plant to blanch the stems, encourage stem rooting, or to provide support. Earthing up potatoes prevents tubers near the soil surface turning green.

Ericaceous (of plants and soil) A lime-hating plant that requires a pH of 6.5 or less to grow, or compost that has a low pH level and is therefore suitable for growing acid-loving plants.

Espalier A tree trained with the main stem vertical and three or four tiers of parallel branches trained out horizontally on a system of wires. Often done with fruit trees.

Evergreen Of plants that retain their leaves for more than one growing season; the foliage usually remains green all year.

Firm in To push the soil down firmly around the rootball of a plant immediately after planting, to prevent it rocking in the wind. Use fingertips to firm in as feet can compact the soil too much.

Flower set Flowers that have been successfully pollinated (usually by insects or the wind) and have produced small fruits.

Force To encourage plant growth early, normally by increasing the temperature. Crops such as sea kale and rhubarb can be forced to produce early and tender crops by excluding light. (See Blanch)

Germination The changes that take place within a seed as it starts to develop into a plant by sending out shoots and roots.

Graft union A bulge low on the trunk where a tree or shrub has been grafted, or joined artificially; a shoot or bud from one plant is joined to the rootstock of another.

Green manure A fast-maturing leafy crop, such as mustard or Phacelia, that is grown to dig into the soil to enrich it.

Grow on To allow a young plant to develop in its pot before planting it outside.

Hardening off Gradually acclimatizing seedlings that have been started off indoors to colder, outdoor conditions; otherwise they could die from the sudden change in temperature.

Herbaceous A non-woody plant that dies down to the rootstock each year at the end of the growing season, then sprouts again the following spring. Usually applied to perennial plants.

High-potash fertilizer A fertilizer that is high in potassium (potash). It encourages plants to produce flowers and fruits, rather than leaves. (See Nitrogen).

Horticultural fleece A special lightweight fabric for covering young or tender plants outside when the weather is cold.

Intercropping The growing of quick-maturing vegetables between slower growing crops to make maximum use of the space available.

Irrigation A general term for watering, or the use of a system of hosepipes and sprinklers to provide water to plants.

Legume A plant in the pea and bean family.

Mulch A material, often well-rotted manure or garden compost, applied in a layer to the soil surface to suppress weeds and retain moisture. Mulching is carried out in early spring around fruit trees and among rows of vegetables.

Nitrogen A soil nutrient that promotes green, leafy growth.

Offset A young plant that grows from the base of the parent plant; it can be severed and grown on as a new plant.

Overwinter To provide protection for tender plants to survive over the winter period. This may entail placing pots in a greenhouse or conservatory, or digging up tubers, (for example, dahlias) and keeping them in a frost-free place.

Pan (in soil) A compacted layer of soil that is impermeable to water and air, and prevents roots from growing properly.

Perennial A plant that lives for more than two years (see Annual and Herbaceous).

pH A measurement used to denote acidity or alkalinity. The scale measures from 1–14; pH7 is neutral, above 7 is alkaline, and below 7 is acid.

Photosynthesis The process whereby a plant converts sunlight and water into energy.

Pilot hole A small hole drilled into a material, or made in the ground, prior to a larger hole being made to hold a screw or a wooden post.

Pinching out The removal of a plant's growing tip to encourage bushier, productive growth.

Planting distance The optimum distance that plants should be spaced at, depending on their eventual height and spread.

Pollination The process by which pollen is transferred during the reproduction of plants, enabling fertilization, and the formation of fruits and seeds.

Potting on Transferring a plant which has outgrown its existing pot into a larger one.

Pricking out Transferring small seedlings from the seed tray or pot in which they germinated to another where they have more room to grow.

Propagation The production of more plants by seeds, cuttings, division, or other methods.

Propagator A heated tray with a lid that maintains a humid atmosphere and encourages newly sown seeds to germinate quickly.

Puddle planting Planting in a hollow to help retain the moisture after watering.

Raised bed A planting bed that is built higher than the surrounding soil, supported by wooden boards, stones, bricks, or other material.

Root nodule A swelling on the root of a leguminous plant, such a pea, that contains bacteria capable of absorbing nitrogen from the air in the soil.

Rootstock A plant used to provide the root system for a grafted plant. Fruit trees are often grafted onto roots that have been specially developed to control the size of the plant.

Rose (of watering can) A perforated cap fitted to the spout of a watering can, causing the water to come out in a gentle spray. Used for seedlings.

Seedling A young plant that emerges after the germination of a seed.

Sequestered iron A special fertilizer to help correct and prevent iron deficiency and the yellowing of leaves. It is given to plants requiring acidic conditions, such as blueberries and cranberries.

Sow direct To sow seeds straight into the soil, usually into a prepared drill. (See Drill)

Successional sowing Sowing seeds little and often in batches so plants are ready to harvest in succession throughout the growing season.

Systemic Describing a pesticide or fungicide that is absorbed and distributed through a plant when applied to the foliage as a spray.

Taproot The main root of a plant, usually thicker and stronger than the lateral roots, and growing straight downward from the stem.

Thinning out The removal of seedlings, shoots, flowers, and fruit buds to improve the growth and quality of those remaining.

Tilth A fine, crumbly surface layer of soil produced by cultivating it thoroughly before sowing seeds.

Topsoil The upper layer of the soil surface. It is usually fertile and good for growing plants.

Transplanting Moving a plant from one position to another.

Tying in Tying wayward shoots to a support structure, such as bamboo canes or posts and wires.

Umbel A flower head that consists of a number of short stalks, which are equal in length and radiate from the stem, like umbrella ribs. It is characteristic of plants such as carrot, dill, fennel, and parsley.

Verticillium wilt A soil-borne fungal disease that results in the yellowing, and eventual browning and death of foliage, particularly in branches closest to the soil. Remove affected plants and soil close to the roots.

Wormery An enclosed unit made from stacked compartments in which compostable materials, such as vegetable peelings, are placed. Special worms turn the waste into compost and liquid fertilizer.

Index

Page numbers in **bold** refer to main entries; page numbers in *italic* refer to illustrations.

Acknowledgements

Picture credits

The publisher would like to thank the following for their kind permission to reproduce their photographs:

Alan Buckingham: 40mc; 43br; 52tl; 53tc; 64mr; 64bl; 70tl; 70ml; 70bl; 72 (all images); 90tc; 90tr; 90ml; 90mr; 90bc; 93bl; 93br; 106-107; 118bcr; 119tr; 130br; 132bl; 136br; 140; 142tr; 148tr; 150; 153mr; 154bc; 156tl; 158bc; 158br; 160tr; 174; 179bcr; 186; 188; 190tr; 191br; 194ml; 195tr; 199tr; 199mr; 202tl; 203bc; 204br; 205tc; 206; 210tr; 211tr; 216tr; 217tr; 218tr; 220tl; 220tr; 221br; 222tr; 222bl; 224br; 226tr; 226bl; 226bc; 226br; 227tl; 227tc; 227tr; 232ml; 232mc; 232mr; 232bl; 232br; 233ml; 233mr; 233bl; 233br; 234tr; 234ml; 235tc; 235br; 236tc; 236tr; 236ml; 236mc; 236bl; 236bc; 237ml; 237mc; 237mr; 240tr; 241tcl; 241tc; 241tcr; 241tr; 242tr; 242br; 244ml; 245tr; 245bcl; 245bcr.

Annabel Akeroyd: 4bl; 7tr; 221tl; Chauney Dunford: 235bc; 236cr; 237bl; Esther Ripley: 230br; Jo Whittingham; 235tl; 235tr; 236br

Dorling Kindersley would like thank:

Illustrations Vanessa Hamilton

Proofreading Angela Baynham

Index Vanessa Bird

The growers at Tudor Allotment Association, Kingston, for allowing us to photograph their wonderful variety of plots, which helped give this book a rich mix of allotment styles.

Boxtrees Nursery Ltd, Walnut Tree Cottage, The Street, Wattisfield, Diss IP22 1NS – for supplying box hedging.

Author's acknowledgement

Firstly I would like to thank May Corfield for working around the clock to translate and edit my passionate horticultural ramblings into something that sounded great. Thank you also to Alison Gardner for her amazing artistic and creative skills, as she made my words look far better than they deserved. A massive thank you to Alex Storch, too, for being a DIY genius who helped transform my allotment from a muddy patch into the envy of all my fellow allotmenteers. Thank you to Helen Bostock at the RHS for her advice, and also to all the staff at DK, particularly Penny Warren, Alison Donovan, and Chauney Dunford for their support and guidance with the book.

Thank you also to my allotment neighbours at Ranmore Allotments, Dorking, Surrey, and particularly Marina Roberts for her support with this project.

Finally I would like to thank my beautiful wife, Annabel, and our three children, Guy, Lissie, and Hugh, for all their support during the summer while I wrote this book – and for enduring a rainy two-week holiday in the Lake District while Daddy locked himself away in a dark room and wrote about vegetables.